Matthew Hosier, Leader, (

This is the most helpful, p[
presents a biblically robust
and equip those who reac
eldership can look like, a
recommend it highly enough.

MW00574233

Alan Frow, Pastor, Southlands Church, U.S.A.

While biblically compelling and inspirational, what sets this book apart
from others on the subject is Smyth's insight into the nuances of elder
team dynamics. From this point of view, there is no other book like it
and it therefore fulfills a significant need for any church pursuing healthy
team leadership. I wholeheartedly commend it to you.

Bob Roberts, Global senior pastor, Northwood Church, U.S.A.

Many years ago, our church went to an elder-led model of leadership. It
was one of the best things we'd ever done. I wish this resource had been
around then! I encourage you to read and absorb this book whether
you're considering the model or strengthening your existing eldership.
It's biblical and practical.

**Bob Thune, Author of *Gospel Eldership*; co-author of *The Gospel-
Centered Life***

If the church is going to thrive and advance, it must be well-led. This
book by PJ Smyth will be a great help toward that end. I'm thankful for
PJ's contribution to the growing body of work on elders, and I pray it
finds a wide readership.

Terry Virgo, Founder of the Newfrontiers movement of churches

Surely few would question the vital role of local churches in God's
plan to glorify his name and make himself known throughout the
world. How those churches are led is not an insignificant matter. In
the volume in your hands, PJ has dug deeply into Scripture and drawn
from considerable personal experience to provide you with a solid and
inspiring workbook to help you build wisely. You would do well to
follow the distilled wisdom that he has worked hard to provide.

Sam Storms, Pastor, Bridgeway Church, U.S.A.

Biblically rooted, theologically rigorous, and eminently practical, this book is a breath of fresh air amidst the ecclesiological fog that often seems to shroud the nature and function of the local church. Smyth speaks incisively and persuasively into the numerous issues of church governance and the dynamics of relationship between the lead pastor and the plurality of male leaders. One need not agree with Smyth on every issue to benefit greatly from his work. In any case, every local church pastor and elder should avail himself of this excellent resource. Highly recommended!

Larry Osborne, Pastor, North Coast Church, U.S.A.

PJ Smyth has written a unique and helpful book on eldership. It's theological, practical, and humble – a rare blend when it comes to the subject. This is not a book written by an idealistic theorist, it's a book built on Scripture and honed in the trenches of real-life ministry. You'll find it helpful both theologically and practically.

Josh Kouri, Lead Pastor, Frontline Church, U.S.A.

This is one of the best books I've read on eldership in the local church. Theologically grounded and full of practical wisdom.

Brett McCracken, Senior Editor at The Gospel Coalition

PJ Smyth's *Elders* is a treasure trove of practical wisdom that should be on the shelf of every elder. It should be read and discussed by every elder team. Drawing first and foremost on Scripture – but also on PJ's many years in the trenches and on the front lines of being an elder himself, and leading/multiplying elders all over the world – this book is a trustworthy and remarkably comprehensive guide. Who are elders according to the Bible? What do they do? How do they function as a healthy team? How do elders relate to the congregation, deacons, staff, and others in the church? These questions and many more are given thorough-yet-concise treatment in this immensely helpful book – truly a gift to the church, both her shepherds and her sheep.

Donnie Griggs, Author of *Small Town Jesus*

Healthy elders lead to healthy churches. Toxic elders lead to toxic churches. No one understands this better than my friend PJ Smyth. In this book we get to learn from PJ's decades of wisdom of personally leading several eldership teams and strengthening countless others all over the world. If you are considering eldership or are already serving as an elder, this book is a must read!

Adrian Warnock, Author of *Hope Reborn* and *Raised With Christ*

PJ is well known for raising up teams of elders wherever he goes. Maybe you want to be a pastor or elder. Or perhaps, like me, you don't. This practical book may help some from each group switch to the other!

Stephen Woodrow, Leader of the G3 Network

This is not just a great practical equipping tool, but a catalyst for developing and multiplying healthy leaders for the Kingdom of God. It is birthed from PJ's many years of living, modeling and advancing these biblical truths. I have personally been the beneficiary of his leadership gift over the years.

Rigby Wallace, Pastor, Common Ground Church, South Africa

After four decades of local church leadership, I regard this book as the finest and fullest summary of eldership. It will arrest complacency and sharpen competency and character. PJ's inspiring work represents a timeless template for followers and leaders alike who are wanting to see elders deployed in a biblical, safe, and dynamic way. If God has called you to be a pastor, read this book. If you're a seasoned pastor, read this book.

Guy Miller, Leader of the Commission movement of churches

For the church to grow, multiply and obey the Great Commission in our 21st century it needs more elders, lots more elders. In this excellent book, PJ gives a clarion call to humble, wise, servant-hearted men to desire this noble task, and provides a full toolbox of theological and practical tools to enable every church to fulfil God's mission.

Joel Virgo, Leader of the Newday Youth Festival

I expect (and hope) that he will write other good books, so I hesitate to say it, but this feels like the book PJ was born to write. Certainly, no one else could. It's clear, compelling, inspiring, timely, brave and reorienting.

And its few pages are filled with more earthy wisdom than many books twice its length.

Mike Betts, Leader of the Relational Mission family of churches

This book provides rich encouragement to the next generation to desire the noble task of eldership. It is an invaluable tool for existing elders to reflect on how they might best put principles into practice in their particular context. I found the study guide particularly helpful in this regard.

Dave Holden, Leader of the New Ground family of churches

I've always loved the privilege of being a local church elder. PJ's outstanding book reminds me why. Refreshing, inspiring, challenging. I love his emphasis that it's the plurality of eldership and not the lone pastor that is so vital for the church today. PJ explains how eldership works in such a thoroughly biblical and yet practical way that will answer many questions. This could radically change your church!

Andy McCullough, Author of *Global Humility*

Elders is written by a practitioner for practitioners. I have visited various churches that PJ has planted over the years, and found healthy eldership teams serving vibrant congregations. This book is thoughtful, straightforward, down-to-earth, robust and inspiring. It will help you, your team, and your church.

John Lanferman, Founder of the Confluence family of churches

A church will never rise above her leadership capacity. *Elders* is a visionary and practical guide to increase that capacity. PJ gives both seasoned and emerging pastors a road map to navigate the vital task of recognizing and developing a dynamic eldership team.

David Devenish, Author of *Succession or Multiplication?* and *Fathering Leaders, Motivating Mission*

Having served on a team with PJ Smyth, I have grown to appreciate his devotion to God, his vision, faith and pastoral wisdom. These characteristics are abundantly illustrated in this excellent book, *Elders*. It conveys clear Biblical teaching accompanied by remarkable practical wisdom and insight. His call for leadership is confident yet humble.

Dr. Mbonisi Malaba, Lead pastor, OneTribe, Kenya

This is jam-packed with leadership gems. The principles in these pages are tried and tested. I have seen PJ teach them and live them out with great effect over twenty years. I heartily commend this book to you.

Steve Tibbert, Senior pastor, King's Church, U.K.

Healthy, growing and vibrant churches are overseen, led and governed well. Healthy eldership teams are integral to this. PJ provides an accessible, practical and challenging book to help us build healthy and effective teams of elders.

Tope Koleoso, Lead pastor, Jubilee Church, U.K.

If the Church in the 21st century is to be all that Jesus intends it to be, it will have to go back to the leadership principles and traditions once handed to us in the Scriptures. With Biblical truth, practical wisdom, and clarity, PJ Smyth shows how elders who will function effectively in their roles can be raised, resourced, and released into their God-appointed calling.

Steve Oliver, Team leader of the Regions Beyond movement of churches

Passion. Theology. Instruction. These are the three words that best describe all that PJ Smyth has packed into this book. For anyone looking to further understand God's leadership order, or for those involved in serving or participating in an eldership team, you will be motivated, equipped and refreshed by this insightful material. I'm so grateful that PJ put this book in my hand – what a great resource to accomplish such a sovereign call!

Jeremy Simpkins, Team leader of the ChristCentral movement of churches

PJ makes a massive contribution to navigating us through the difficult waters of local church eldership. With biblical grace and practical skill, he equips elders to recognize, train and release more elders. It's obvious that PJ has not learned these truths in the comfort of a study, but he has lived them out on the reality of the battlefield. I'd encourage every church leadership to work through this book together.

Sheshi Kaniki, Lead elder, God's Tribe Church, Tanzania

PJ Smyth has written an excellent book that is highly inspiring and full of practical wisdom. It speaks to the heart and the mind. It has equipped me for this noble task. I am convinced it will also equip you.

Scott Marques, Team leader of the DnA movement of churches

PJ has a unique ability for inspiration through thorough yet concise communication. He is a joy to learn from. Authentic and packed with coalface experience, this book outlines the core principles of eldership health that have yielded fruit in his own life and in many multiplying churches over many years. Any elder, or aspiring elder, will do well to read and internalize this from cover to cover.

Bishop Edward Buria, Leader of the Kerith Church Movement, Kenya

Get it and read it! *Elders* is rich in biblical application, godly wisdom and real-life experience. It answers many questions on how to have a godly, healthy, and missional eldership.

Dr. Andrew Butterworth, Pastor, GodFirst Church, East Rand, South Africa

PJ Smyth has mastered the craft of eldership. After decades as a church pioneer and leader, he's put all his gems into this potent book. Dripping with theology and application, each chapter concludes with questions to stimulate discussion. It's ideal for training up new elders *and* sharpening the knowledge and practice of existing ones. While rooted in great exegesis, this is no ivory-tower tome. It has been forged in the hustle and bustle of real church life. It is comprehensive but straight to the point. Do your church a favor; don't just get a copy for yourself, get copies for all your leaders. It's the only book on eldership you'll ever need.

Corey Sanders, Lead pastor, Movement Church, U.S.A.

As a church planter, I have read a plethora of books on eldership, and this is the most practical and relevant eldership guide. PJ's content is concise and manageable for both readers and small groups. He addresses the quality of spiritual life an elder must embody and the importance of camaraderie as faithful men serve alongside one another. I believe this book will serve as an excellent tool for discipleship training for those aspiring to hold the office of elder and a useful resource for discipling men in the congregation.

Steve Van Rhyn, Pastor, Jubilee Church, South Africa

If you are looking for a book on eldering that is full of grit, passion, inspiration and road-tested wisdom, look no further. I first met PJ Smyth and his first eldership team in January 2000 at River of Life Church in Harare, Zimbabwe. For the last 20 years I have seen an unrelenting passion in PJ to see eldership teams get established, get healthy, and get growing. PJ has forged eldership teams in multiple church plants and large, complex multi-site churches in three different countries. The book you are holding isn't the musings of an armchair critic but the hard-won learnings of a wise master builder with the scars to prove it.

ELDERS

Developing Elders & Revitalizing Teams

BY PJ SMYTH

Published by **Advance**

Published by Advance
3 London Road, Redhill, RH1 1LY, United Kingdom,
www.advancemovement.com

ISBN 978-1-9163691-6-0 (paperback)
ISBN 978-1-9163691-7-7 (e-book)

All italicizations in scripture passages have been added by the author.
A catalogue record of this book is available from the British Library.

Cover Design by Nathan Lambert
Typeset in Adobe Garamond Pro and Brandon Grotesque

DEDICATION

To Scott Marques and Derek Landman,
the first two elders I served with.

Twenty-five years ago, we started to write this book.

OTHER BOOKS BY PJ SMYTH

Crossing the Line of Faith

A short book for churches to give to people who are considering crossing the line of faith, or who recently have.

Through the Waters of Baptism

A short book for churches to give to people who are considering getting baptized, or who recently have.

How the Gospel Moves from Friend to Friend

Suitable for individuals or small groups who want to be evangelistically effective every day.

CONTENTS

ACKNOWLEDGEMENTS

Profound thanks to the various eldership teams I have led over the years. We wrote this book together. Thanks also to my wife Ashleigh, and Jack, Ben and Sam for your love and support. Thanks to my publishing team of Phil Whittall, Jennie Pollock, and Nathan Lambert.

FOREWORD BY ANDREW WILSON

This is the best book on eldership I have ever read.

Books on this subject are usually written by two sorts of people. There are *thinkers*: academics and scholars who walk us through what the Bible says from a theoretical perspective (like many of my favourite writers). And there are *thinker-doers*: people who serve as part of an eldership team somewhere, and participate in the government of the church, but whose primary gift is still clearly on the intellectual and theoretical side (like me). Both types of book can be helpful, but both tend to address questions that are more conceptual than practical, and may contain plenty of insight but not much fire. (*Doers*, by and large, are so busy being elders that they don't have time to write books about it.) What we need is a book about eldership from a *doer-thinker*: someone who can challenge us biblically and provoke us intellectually, but whose gifts and contribution primarily revolve around leadership, wisdom, application and experience. We need someone who will speak to us as if we are about to enter a pasture, or even a battlefield (Acts 20:25-31), rather than a library.

This is what PJ has provided. This book does not simply answer the usual questions in a different way; it asks different questions. What does it actually mean to have a team of equals where one of them is the leader? How do fathers and mothers serve together in the church? How do you train and reproduce elders? What sorts of things stop eldership teams from functioning properly, and what can we do about them? These are the issues that we wrestle with each week, and they are addressed here with clarity, honesty, biblical insight and passion. The result is a book that feels more like a travel guide than an atlas, which eldership teams of all shapes and sizes will benefit from working through together.

In his opening paragraph, PJ makes a striking statement: "I don't want to be a rock star, a fighter pilot or an astronaut. I want to be an elder." You can tell. The vision he casts is compelling, and you can smell its authenticity, because it is borne out of a life spent pastoring God's people in three different countries. So even when readers disagree with PJ on exactly how to answer some of the questions he raises, my guess is that few will dismiss the importance of asking them, nor the integrity, humour and robustly biblical common sense with which he responds.

Anyway: I am grateful to God, and to PJ, for this book. I trust that you will be too.

HOW TO USE THIS BOOK

I enjoy most aspects of leading a church, but none more than leading an eldership team and developing new elders. This book has emerged out of nearly twenty-five years of eldership experience, and is designed to help *develop* potential elders and *recalibrate* existing elders.

Each chapter concludes with a *reflection section* to help the reader engage with the material and facilitate group discussion. The questions probe the heart and help clarify ministry philosophy, and press the reader to apply what he is learning in the context of his eldership team and church.

The structure of the book allows *flexibility* in how it can be used. *Potential elders* could meet with an existing elder(s) to discuss their answers to the reflection section of each chapter. *Existing elders* might work through the book together, discussing their answers in each reflection section.

The "feel" of the book is somewhere between a text book and a motivational leadership book. To keep the book to a manageable length and to keep the momentum up, I avoid unnecessary padding and have been restrained with personal anecdotes. I have bucked the modern trend of starting each chapter with an attention-grabbing story as I know most elders and potential elders are busy people, and I trust they will appreciate the no-nonsense approach.

I usually quote Scripture references within the text rather than as footnotes to assist ease of reference for those who will read this book with their Bibles open. All Scriptures are quoted in the English Standard Version unless otherwise specified, and all italics and bold in quoted verses are mine.

PART 1

FOUNDATIONS

Elders

CHAPTER 1
MEN WITH VISION

Elders are explosively dangerous men as far as the kingdom of darkness is concerned. They are warrior brothers dedicated to Jesus and his church, and champions of gospel advance in their neighborhoods and the nations.

PRIVILEGE

I enjoy good movies. I am stirred watching Maximus Meridius lead his men in a fight to the death in the Coliseum. I am roused watching Louis Zamperini inspire his fellow prisoners in the face of extraordinary cruelty. But nothing excites me more than leading our church into the purposes of God with my fellow elders. I don't want to be a rock star, a fighter pilot or an astronaut. I want to be an elder.

My journey to eldership got off to a dubious start. In 1997, aged 25, I started a church with my wife and twelve friends who were unhinged enough to give it a go. A few months in, I appointed myself and two of my best friends as elders. I just announced it. Appointing elders can be so easy when you do it wrong! About a year later, we connected with a movement of churches called Newfrontiers, who took us under their wing and coached us in all-things church, including eldership. As we learned from the Bible what elders really were, our faces became redder and redder, and the three of us decided to de-elder ourselves. We asked our friends in Newfrontiers to help our congregation find suitable men to appoint in our place, or to reappoint us if and when appropriate. We were soon reappointed, and by God's grace went on to become a healthy eldership team.

I have now been an elder for nearly twenty-five years. The first eight years (1997 to 2004) were in River of Life Church in Zimbabwe, and the next twelve (2005 to 2016) were in GodFirst Church in South Africa. My wife and I planted both of these churches, which both grew steadily and became multi-congregational churches. We gained a great deal of experience with eldership teams because our model was to develop eldership teams for each of the congregations as they gradually matured into their own autonomous churches.

From 2017 to 2018 I did a two-year stint at Covenant Life Church in the metro area of Washington D.C. After several years of significant challenges in the church, the hope was that I would be able to help the elders swing the eldership pendulum to the "dynamic middle" where the strengths of a leader and the strengths of a team converge. The pendulum proved more resistant than we anticipated, but they were two valuable years in fine-tuning my convictions around eldership. Since 2019, I have been leading the eldership team at Monument Church (which we planted), and continuing to strengthen eldership teams around the world.

Being an elder for nearly my entire adult life has been a massive privilege. Despite challenges along the way, I wouldn't trade it for anything. Being on the frontlines of local church life and leadership with a team of brothers has been riveting and invigorating. Together, we have fasted and prayed, celebrated, mourned, confessed our faith, and sometimes confessed our sin. We have made audacious, faith-fueled decisions together. We have charged mountains together. And we have laughed and laughed together.

Several moments stand out for me, such as when Scott Marques and Derek Landman (fellow elders on my first eldership team in Zimbabwe) sat me down and asked me if I was aware how unpleasant I could sometimes be to follow! They spoke truth to me, with love, that made it easier for me to hear the hard news. They pointed out that I was sometimes more passionate about the project than the people, which could make it feel like I was using people more than serving people. I was cut to the heart, but I felt deeply cared for by those two brothers. By God's grace, I am told I have improved in this regard since then.

Another memorable moment came when praying with Stephen Jack, Greg Tait and Sheshi Kaniki (the first group of elders at GodFirst Church in South Africa). We experienced something of an Acts 13 moment, where we clearly felt God commission Stephen and Greg to lead their own congregations, which led us into multi-site. The presence of God was tangible. It was one of the most genuinely prophetic moments I have been part of. In fact, many of my sweetest memories of eldership have been in times of prayer together.

When I was diagnosed with cancer in 2010, I had to step out of leading the church for nearly a year while I received treatment. Eldership plurality serves a local church in many ways, not least to secure her in the event of the leader being taken out. Over that year, neither the congregation that I led nor the wider multi-congregational church missed a beat because we were a church led by elders – *a team with a leader* more than *a leader with a team*. Another crisis hit me in 2017 when I was falsely accused of various things. I was privileged to have my eldership team investigate the matter, and clear me of wrong-doing. Rather than having to defend myself, it was a privilege to be accountable to a respected, duly elected body of brothers who could objectively weigh the accusation against me.

My family has also felt the privilege of eldership. Ashleigh has known a better husband because I have been an elder. Jack, Ben and Sam have known a better dad because I have been an elder. Simply, I have found eldership to be a disciple-making, man-shaping, family-blessing privilege. I became an elder by the calling and grace of God. I remain an elder by the calling and grace of God. And, by God's grace, I pray this book will help other men discover this same calling and grace.

CRISIS AND OPPORTUNITY

As much as I long for more and more men to enjoy the personal benefits of eldership, I have a higher motivation for writing this book: the Great Commission. If we are to fulfil Christ's mandate to take the gospel to our generation, we need to plant thousands of churches across the nations of the world in the coming decades. For this to be done *well*, we need more leaders at every level of the local church. For this to be done *at all*, we need more elders. Loads. More. Elders.

The world needs more of *Jesus*, therefore it needs more *churches*, therefore it needs more *elders*. A church can operate without a building, without an office, without a cappuccino machine, without musicians, without all manner of ministries, but it cannot operate without elders, at least not for long.

I was told I would sell more books if I entitled this book *Leaders*, because apparently the leadership market is enormous, whereas the elder market is small. My point exactly. The rate of conversion from *leader* to *elder* is way too slow. We need all sorts of leaders, with all sorts of gifts, in all sorts of roles in the church, and of course not everyone is called by God to be an elder. Yet the crisis remains: we are not producing elders fast enough and well enough. We need a new generation of men to hear the call to eldership, and to humbly and courageously respond. To my mind, three main things contribute to the scarcity of elders today: a deficit of character, a deficit of courage, and a deficit of vision.

CHARACTER

General Norman Schwarzkopf said if a man had to choose between leadership and character, he should choose the latter.[1] So too with elders. When I started out in ministry, I would say things like "character is more important than gifting" but I am not sure I really believed it. I believe it now. I believe it because over the years I have watched many elders drop out of the race. Some have re-joined, although they and their teams bear the scars. Some will never run again. The thing is, not one of them dropped out due to a deficit of gifting, courage or vision.

Brothers, each of us is just one foolish decision away from disqualification, and we make such decisions based on character not gifting. Character is so important that the flagship passages about eldership in Scripture are devoted mostly to issues of character. We devote an entire section of this book (Part 6) to a study of these passages. Three whole chapters. I am leaving it to the latter part of the book not because it is less important, but because you will feel a growing sense of its importance with each piece of the eldership calling we describe throughout the book. With that growing awareness in place, we'll drive home the key character traits that Scripture and experience indicate must be strong in a thriving elder.

COURAGE

Eldership requires courage, yet courage is not in vogue. Edwin H. Friedman notes that modern culture, certainly in the West, is generally cynical about leadership courage:

> I believe there exists throughout America today a rampant sabotaging of leaders who try to stand tall amid the raging anxiety-storms of our time … a regressive mood that contaminates the decision-making processes of government and corporations at the highest level, and, on the local level, seeps down into the deliberations of neighborhood church, synagogue, hospital, library, and school boards.[2]

Ironically, America exists *because* of leadership courage. She was founded on the mettle of the explorers, fashioned by the resolve of the Founding Fathers, and forged by the valor of American soldiers on multiple battlefields. And yet, today American culture is generally risk-averse, leadership-dissenting, and adventure-shy. It is the same in Africa. In Zimbabwe, the famous reply given by anyone who is blamed for anything is, "I am not the one" – do you hear echoes of Adam in Eden? The Adamic propensity to abdicate is alive and well in our generation, making it hard for elders to lead as they should. Of course, elders should be servant-hearted and Christ-like not insensitive or dictatorial, but leading with courage is essential. Elders need to settle up front that eldership is not for the faint-hearted. James Stewart writes:

> Field-Marshal Wavell has told, in his notable lectures entitled *Generals and Generalship*, the story of how

> Napoleon, when an artillery officer at the siege of Toulon, built a battery in such an exposed position that he was told he would never find men to man it. But Napoleon had a sure instinct for what was required. He put up a placard – 'The battery of men without fear': and it was always manned![3]

Eldership is an exposed position, and courageous men are required to man it.

VISION

Three men were laying bricks together. A passer-by asked each man what he was doing. The first said, "I am laying a brick." The second said, "I am building a wall." The third said, "I am building a great cathedral." I have found that elders generally think about eldership in similar categories. Most are in the first group, some are in the second, and a minority in the third.

The first group think of eldership as "laying a brick." They draw their job description exclusively from New Testament texts that specifically mention the characteristics and function of elders, including 1 Timothy 3, Titus 1, 1 Peter 5, and Acts 20. They rightly conclude from these texts that elders should be men of godly *character* who *shepherd* and *teach* their congregation.

The second group think of eldership as "building a wall." They draw their job description from the same texts as the previous group, but also from what the New Testament teaches more broadly about the nature and purpose of the local church. They reason, "If elders are called to lead New Testament-style churches, and if New Testament churches were clearly spirit-filled, prayerful, evangelistic, city-impacting communities, then it follows that elders should be spirit-filled, prayerful, evangelistic, city-impacting men." Hence, their vision for eldership is larger and better than the first group.

The third group of elders, the "cathedral builders," think about eldership the same way as the second group, yet their vision for eldership is grander still. They note how the entirety of Scripture presents the people of God as joining God in his mission to bring his knowledge and glory to all the nations of the earth (Gen. 12:1-3 through Rev. 7:9-12). They note how Jesus commissioned the Church to global evangelization (Matt. 28:18-20, Acts 1:8). And consequentially, they reason that elders should be men committed to this grand, global vision for their generation. Although the majority of their time and energy likely goes into mobilizing their church for *neighborhood* mission, if you cut them, these men bleed with a grand vision for gospel evangelization of the *nations*.

Certainly, elders should display the basic character and competencies laid out in the "brick" texts of the New Testament, but in terms of defining eldership, we don't start there. That would be like an actor learning his lines and developing his character before finding out about the grand theme of the production.

Jesus leaves us in no doubt about the ultimate aim of local church life:

> But you will receive power when the Holy Spirit has come upon you, and you will be my witnesses in Jerusalem and in all Judea and Samaria, and to the end of the earth. (Acts 1:8)

That is the mission of God, therefore *that* is the mission of the Church, therefore that is the mission of elders. If elders interpret their role *outside* of the Great Commission, they reduce the office of elder to something much scantier than God intended. But if elders interpret their role inside the Great Commission, the basic "bricklaying" of eldership gets infused with a "Cathedral-building" largesse and energy otherwise quite unattainable. The basics of eldership – modelling godly character, caring for people, and teaching God's word – are now done on a trajectory of pushing back darkness in their neighborhoods and the nations. If big vision attracts big men, then "cathedral building" eldership will attract giants.

To use a maritime metaphor, if you strip the Great Commission *out of* eldership, then a local church is merely a barge tied up to a pier. It's a nice barge with two main living areas. One is a hospital where the elders *care* for the saints, and the other is a classroom where the elders *teach* the saints. They teach the saints to keep their cabins tidy and to perform various tasks on the barge. Everyone seems well cared for and well taught, but the barge stays tied up to the pier. It never goes anywhere. It never makes any waves.

Conversely, when you inject the Great Commission *into* eldership, then a local church becomes a battleship on the high seas. It also has a hospital area below deck where injured saints are cared for, and there is also a classroom where the saints are equipped. But those in the hospitable recuperate to the background throb of the propellers driving the ship forward, and they sleep with a gun under their pillow. Those in the classroom are taught to the sound of the guns on deck blasting away at the kingdom of darkness, and when class ends they are back on deck. The context of care and training is mission. The theatre is war. The trajectory is forward. When elders locate their calling within the Great Commission, they become explosively dangerous men as far as the kingdom of darkness is concerned – warrior brothers, dedicated to Jesus, devoted to the local church, and champions of gospel advance in the neighborhoods and nations.

REFLECTION

1. Why do you aspire to eldership?

2. What aspects of eldership most excite you and which most concern you?

3. On a scale of 1 to 5 (with 5 being "high"), how would you describe your level of courage for eldership? Briefly elaborate.

4. In terms of the three bricklayers, which group do you think you are in? Briefly elaborate.

5. Is your church a barge or a battleship? Briefly elaborate.

Elders

CHAPTER 2

MEN WITH SCARS

There is no place in the ranks of elders for those who suppose they can shepherd in a way that Jesus didn't – without startling loss to earthly ambition and carnage to natural desire. A call to eldership is a call to come and die.

We are told to work out our salvation with fear and trembling (Phil. 2:12-13). This chapter is the *fear and trembling* moment for potential elders, and a sober reminder for existing elders. I pray that God would use this chapter to drive many men away from eldership, and some toward it. As the Lord sifted Gideon's army at the spring of Harod, may he sift the readers of this book, and filter out the scar-averse. Jesus *gave himself up* for the church (Eph. 5:25), therefore, there is no place in the ranks of elders for those who suppose they can shepherd in a way that Jesus didn't – without startling loss to earthly ambition and carnage to natural desire. Eldership is the road less traveled, and potential travelers must first count the cost. Jesus said:

> If anyone comes to me and does not hate his own father and mother and wife and children and brothers and sisters, yes, and even his own life, he cannot be my disciple. Whoever does not bear his own cross and come after me cannot be my disciple. For which of you, desiring to build a tower, does not first sit down and count the cost, whether he has enough to complete it? (Lk. 14:26-27).

Elders are called to exemplify "normal" Christianity. Therefore, if every Christian should count the cost in this way, how much more should elders? Could it be that the general lack of sacrifice amongst Christians today has been propagated by a general lack of sacrifice amongst elders? Potential elders should count the cost in the following areas:

THE COST OF DISCIPLESHIP

If you are considering eldership, you cannot say, "Lord, I am happy to serve you, but on my terms. Let us go 50-50 on this: you get my service, but I get to choose the conditions of that service." Did Jesus say, "If anyone would come after me, let him negotiate his terms, deny difficulty, and stand up for his rights?" Or did he say, "If anyone would come after me, let him deny himself and take up his cross daily and follow me" (Luke 9:23)? Elders must clearly see the absurdity of trying to negotiate terms with the One who "also made the stars" (Gen. 1:16 NIV). Elders have settled, completely settled, that they cannot serve God *and* Money, or God *and* Self, or God *and* Comfort. In *The Man God Uses*, Oswald J. Smith writes:

> Now let us ask ourselves some very plain questions. Does God come first in my life or does business hold the supreme place? Is it God first or pleasure? God first or money? What about my family, my loved ones? Do they come first or does God? What then, are the terms of discipleship? Let me give the answer in just two words: "GOD FIRST". And if I could, I would put them on a banner in the sight of every congregation in the world – GOD FIRST.[4]

If you have invited Jesus into your life to improve it rather than rule it, don't become an elder. If you want him to bless your agenda rather than making his agenda your only agenda, don't become an elder. If you claim to have entered his Kingdom, but are actually hoping that he will enter yours, don't become an elder. If you call him savior but treat him like a service-provider, don't become an elder. If your terms of discipleship are anything other than GOD FIRST, do not become an elder.

THE COST OF THE TITUS STEP

In J.R.R. Tolkien's novel, *The Hobbit*, Bilbo Baggins pleads, "I just need to sit quietly for a moment." Gandalf responds, "You've been sitting quietly for far too long!" Men in your twenties and thirties, listen to me: if you sit quietly for too long, somewhere between the age of thirty-five and forty-five you will, in a flash, go from being that "great young guy with great potential" to that "middle-aged guy who hasn't done anything." To avoid this sorry state of affairs, you need to take the step that few take. I call it the "Titus Step." Paul describes it in 2 Corinthians 8:16-17, 23:

> I thank God, who put into the heart of Titus the same concern I have for you. For Titus not only welcomed our appeal, but he is coming to you with much enthusiasm and on his own initiative.... As for Titus, he is my partner and fellow worker among you. (NIV)

Did you spot the magic words: *His. Own. Initiative.* He received from God his *own* concern for the church. He stopped riding the coat tails of Paul's enthusiasm and initiative, and developed his *own*. That was how he transitioned from being Paul's junior to Paul's "partner and fellow worker." Don't step into eldership before you have stepped into ownership. Before ordaining you, the elders must say to themselves, "Something has happened in that man's heart. The freeloader has become a load bearer. The hired hand has become a shepherd. Now he won't run when the wolf comes, for he owns the sheep in his heart. He is truly our partner and fellow worker" (see John 10:11-15).

THE COST OF TRUE FORTUNE

Those who lead in the Kingdom of God must be clear on what is "up" and what is "down," for things are different there from the kingdom of man. Spurgeon explains the difference:

> Have you a better house than you used to have, and more money, more friends, and more of this world's good things; and do you now forget your God? Ah, then you have indeed gone down in the world.… If you had come to me and told me that you had lost everything, but that you loved Jesus better, I should have sympathized with you because of your trouble, but I should have congratulated you on your fortune. But now that you have got on so well in the world that you do not love your Lord as you once did, I can only pity you because of your dreadful poverty and mourn over the fearful loss that you have experienced.[5]

If the things you own actually own you, eldership is not for you.

THE COST OF HARDSHIPS AHEAD

The Bible mentions many wonderful things that are ours in Christ. We are created in Christ, chosen in Christ, redeemed in Christ, recipients of every spiritual blessing in Christ, and ultimately, we shall be raised in Christ (Eph. 2:10, 1:4, 1:7, 1:3, 1 Cor. 15:22). Yet, we also share in the suffering of Christ. The apostles agree on this: John introduces himself as, "your brother and companion in the suffering and kingdom and patient endurance that are ours in Jesus" (Rev. 1:9 NIV). Paul concurred that every heir of God and co-heir with Christ will share in his suffering and his glory, and that both the sufferings and the comfort of Christ overflow into our lives (Rom. 8:17, 2 Cor. 1:5, Phil. 3:10). Peter tells us not to be surprised at hardships, and calls us to rejoice as we participate in Christ's sufferings (1 Pet. 4:12-13). If hardship is to be anticipated by the rank and file in God's army, then it is guaranteed for elders, for elders are called to exemplify normal Christianity. In any case, officers always draw more enemy fire than the troops. Yet this has benefits, for pastors who have suffered are better able to pastor those who suffer (2 Cor. 1:3-5). John Newton explains:

> God appoints his ministers to be sorely exercised, both from without and within; that they may sympathize with their flock, and know in their own hearts the deceitfulness of sin, the infirmities of the flesh, and the way in which the Lord supports and bears all who trust in Him. The leader benefits, and everyone benefits.[6]

Brothers, God will strengthen you through every storm (Ps. 139:5-8, Isa. 50:10, Matt. 28:20, Rom. 8:38-39, Heb. 13:5), but if storms are not for you, then don't become an elder.

THE COST OF LIFE

A fundamental role that elders play is *protector*. In the New Testament era, a shepherd (a common biblical description of elders) was a dangerous profession. As Jesus said in John 10, fighting off robbers and wolves, and being prepared to lay down their life for the flock, was a serious expectation for a shepherd. The New Testament era was one of significant persecution and suffering for the early church, similar to certain countries today. I have friends, and friends of friends, around the world today who are elders, and they are the first to be taken in for questioning, or imprisoned. Although in many parts of the world elders may not be at risk of imprisonment or death from persecution, at the time of writing the globe is gripped by the COVID-19 pandemic, and elders who care for congregants who are sick and dying will experience some risk to their health. Apart from the risks of persecution and health, elders are often the first to be targeted by social or mainstream media, and just one disgruntled congregant can cause reputational damage. Elders are protectors, and this cost should be counted.

THE COST THAT CHRIST PAID

Where might we find grace to joyfully embrace the cost of eldership? At the cross. In Acts 20:28, Paul charged the Ephesian elders "to care for the church of God" and he then added, by way of ultimate motivation, "which he obtained with his own blood." He called on them to remember the cross of Christ, knowing that at the cross the cost of eldership becomes the *privilege* of eldership. Ann Voskamp writes:

[God] gave us Jesus. Jesus! Gave him up for us all. If we have only one memory, isn't this one enough? Why is this the memory I most often take for granted? He cut open the flesh of the God-Man and let the blood. He washed our grime with the bloody grace…. Doesn't that memory alone suffice? Need there be anything more? … The bark on the raw wounds, the thorns pressed into the brow, your name on the cracked lips … He has … given us the incomprehensible.[7]

Brothers, remember the cross. Remember Christ who gave himself for the church (Eph. 5:25). Remember our Shepherd who laid down his life for the sheep (Jn. 10:11). Allow this *one great memory* to melt your heart into a Christ-like form, into a shepherd-like shape, and empower you for eldership.

Like Chuck Palahniuk, author of *Fight Club*, potential elders must be able to say, "I don't want to die without any scars." If they can't, they should not become elders. Amy Carmichael, missionary to India for fifty-five years, wrote:

> *Hast thou no scar?*
> *No hidden scar on foot, or side, or hand?*
> *I hear thee sung as mighty in the land,*
> *I hear them hail thy bright ascendant star:*
> *Hast thou no scar?*
>
> *No wound? No scar?*
> *Yet, as the Master shall the servant be,*
> *And piercèd are the feet that follow Me;*
> *But thine are whole: can he have followed far*
> *Who has no wound nor scar?*[8]

Remember him. Remember his scars. Like Thomas, place your hand in his side and your finger in his hands and feet, and say, "My Lord and my God!"

REFLECTION

This is a defining chapter of the book, and possibly a defining moment in your life. Write a short paragraph with your reflections on these things:

- The cost of discipleship

- The cost of the Titus Step

- The cost of true fortune

- The cost of hardships ahead

- The cost that Christ paid

Elders

CHAPTER 3
POLITY, PLURALITY, AND AUTHORITY

Eldership teams minimize the weaknesses and amplify the strengths of the individual members. Few burdens seem heavy when everyone lifts. Few enemies seem intimidating with brothers at your side. Few fortresses seem unassailable when you charge them together.

ORIGINS

Elders were an important part of the governmental structure in Old Testament Israel. Although they are mentioned over one hundred times in the Old Testament, we are not given details of how they governed, how they were chosen, how old they were, or what qualifications they had. There were different types of elders such as elders of Israel (Ex. 3:16), of tribes (Deut. 31:28) and of cities (Deut. 19:12). The elders worked closely with other leadership groups including officials (Deut. 31:28), judges (Deut. 21:2), heads of tribes (Deut. 5:23), family chiefs (1 Kings 8:1) and priests (1 Kings 8:3). The nation of Israel continued this kind of leadership layout into the era of Jesus and the early church, although by this time groups such as Pharisees, chief priests and teachers of the law were also in play (Matt. 15:2, 16:21, Acts 4:8).

The first time we encounter the word "elder" in the New Testament is Acts 11:30. Luke, the author of Acts, doesn't tell us why or how the leaders of the early church came to use the term "elder," or how the first elders in Jerusalem were appointed. We assume that from Acts 2 to Acts 11 the apostles led the Jerusalem church, and that by Acts 11, inspired by the Holy Spirit, they adopted the term "elder" from the Old Testament and Jewish culture to designate the group of men who led the local church. Maybe some (or all) of the apostles continued to serve as elders. Certainly, Peter appeared to happily own the role of elder throughout his apostolic ministry (1 Pet. 5:1), but it seems that others who were not apostles were appointed as additional elders (Acts 15:8). Whatever the process was, "We can be sure that the establishment of congregational oversight by a plurality of elders was no arbitrary decision."[9]

From Acts 11:30 onwards, elder-led congregations were clearly the norm. In Acts 14:23, we read of Paul and Barnabas appointing elders in "every church" that they had started. In Acts 15 and 16, we read of the Jerusalem elders interacting with the apostles on a matter of doctrine. In Acts 20, Paul meets with the Ephesian elders in Miletus. And, in Acts 21:18, we hear again about the Jerusalem elders.

In the epistles, there are various references to elders. Paul's letter to the Philippians is addressed to the elders and others (1:1). The three main lists of elders' characteristics are found in 1 Timothy 3:1-13, Titus 1:5-9 and 1 Peter 5:1-4, and there are also significant things said about elders in Acts 20, 1 Timothy 4:14, 5:17-19, 1 Thessalonians 5:12-13, James 5:13-15, and Hebrews 13:7 and 17. (I believe these references to "leaders" in Hebrews 13 are referring to elders, or similar.[10]) Also, the apostle John referred to himself as "the elder" in the opening verses of 2 John and 3 John.

The last we hear of elders in the Bible concerns the twenty-four elders around the heavenly throne (Rev. 4:4). They seem to be a type of high council, either representatives of the eternal body of Christ, or angels, yet they bear the title "elder." It is a remarkable thing that elders have their history in the Old and New Testaments, and their future in heaven where the title "elder" will live on into eternity describing the twenty-four elders around the throne.

TERMINOLOGY

The Bible uses three words interchangeably to describe the same office: *presbuteros* (which is most commonly translated "elder"), *poimen* ("pastor/shepherd"), and *episkopos* ("overseer/bishop").

31

Paul uses the words "*presbuteros*" and "*episkopos*" interchangeably in Acts 20:17 and Acts 20:28, and in Titus 1:5 and Titus 1:7. Peter does likewise with all three terms in 1 Peter 5:1-2. Therefore, we may conclude that elders are pastors/shepherds, who are also overseers. Maybe part of the reason for the interchange is to capture something of their dignified *position* (elder), as well as something of their *function* (overseers, shepherds). There seems to be no biblical distinction between the role of an elder and a bishop, although some denominations use the two words to describe different offices.

So, what should we call elders? Biblically speaking, it seems we *could* call them elders, pastors, shepherds, overseers, or even bishops. I prefer the term "elders" for the following reasons:

- "Elders" is the most frequently used biblical term to describe those who lead a church.[11]

- "Elders" better emphasizes the plurality of the office in cultures that are prone to get over-enamored with "the pastor."

- "Elders" better accommodates the breadth of gifting that elders may have. Minimally, all elders should be pastorally gifted, but each may have different gifts besides that, sometimes pronounced gifts, and always and only referring to him as "pastor" can be somewhat limiting.

- Always calling the elders "pastors" can over-emphasize the pastoral aspect of church life to the neglect of other important aspects, such as evangelism.

- Some cults have hijacked the term "elder" and use it in unbiblical ways. It is a title we should fight for, not surrender.

Notwithstanding my personal preference for the title "elder," the advantage of having different biblical phrases to describe the same office is that the chances are one of them will suit your context and culture. Whatever title you choose as your predominant term, I suggest you *clearly explain* what you mean by it, and then be *consistent in your usage*. For example, some churches call elders who are on the church staff "pastors," and call elders who are not on the church staff "elders." Assuming the two groups are actually one-and-the-same in terms of your ecclesiology and structure, then why not rather call them by the same title (noun) preceded by a simple adjective, such as "staff elders" and "non-staff elders?" Doing so helps mitigate against people thinking that elders and pastors are two different offices in the Bible, or that earning a salary from the church somehow makes an elder more of an elder, or less of an elder, than those who earn a salary from somewhere else.

POLITY

There seem to be three main forms of church government in operation today:

Episcopacy

Episcopacy means "ruled by bishops." This is a top-down model in which a senior leader (maybe an archbishop) has authority over the second-tier leaders (maybe bishops), who each have authority over local churches in a geographical area (maybe called a district or diocese). A priest of some sort (maybe a vicar) leads each congregation in the district. Although this model of oversight is not obvious in Scripture, the rationale is that it continues the form of church government that some believe the early church had evolved into by the time the original apostles died off. The logical progression thereafter was for successors to appoint subsequent successors.

This model is not without strengths, although it seems that rather than bishops, it should be the prerogative of *local elders* and *trusted outside ministers* to recognize and appoint local church leaders (Acts 13:1-3, Acts 14:23, 1 Tim. 4:14). Part of the reason to prefer this approach is that the term "bishop" is biblically synonymous with the term "pastor/elder/overseer." "Bishop" does not seem to indicate a "higher order" of leader.

Presbyterianism

Presbyterianism means "ruled by *presbyters*," which is the Greek word for "elders." In this system of polity, local elders who are resident in that local church lead the church. However, denominational Presbyterianism places another layer (or more) of governance over the local church in the form of synods or general assemblies, which are *higher* groups of elders that preside over a group of churches.

The Acts 15 assembly of "apostles and elders" lends some credence to this kind of polity, although one should be cautious about reading too much into what was a unique situation between two churches. The conclusions of the council do not necessarily imply that the Jerusalem elders had authority over the Antioch church, or any other church. Whilst the Jerusalem elders certainly helped shape doctrine for their church and the Antioch church, it was arguably the apostle Paul who elevated that local ruling to a wider ruling (Acts 16:4). Either way, it seems to be a stretch to say that Acts 15 is the equivalent to a modern-day synod of elders making formal decrees for all churches, especially when this model of polity is not obvious elsewhere in the New Testament.

The greatest strength of this system is its conclusion that local elders govern local churches, a conclusion this book will argue has immense biblical support. However, biblical support for regional elder boards (synods) that oversee local church congregations is harder to find. Certainly, the plurality of pluralities (the combination of local church elders and the regional synod) makes for robust accountability, although an imposed external governing body often struggles to produce genuine unity, and a multi-tiered form of government is complex in nature and tends to disempower those in the bottom tier.

Congregationalism

Congregationalism refers to local churches that are congregationally governed, usually meaning two things. First, it means that the church is *self-governed*, ultimately answerable to itself rather than an individual, synod, or denomination beyond the church. Second, it means that it is *democratically governed*, meaning that the congregation is the highest authority rather than an individual (such as a senior pastor), or a group (such as a board of elders).

Proponents of congregationalism would point out that Jesus seemed to imply this model of church government in Matthew 18 when he told us to take even the most extreme disagreements to *the church* rather than the bishop, synod, apostolic team, elders or deacons.

Conclusions

As I will argue below under the headings *Plurality* and *Authority*, I believe Scripture presents leadership *authority* in a local church lying with a *plurality* of elders *within* that congregation, rather than with the congregation or with some external entity. According to the definitions above, this would be something of a blend of Presbyterianism and Congregationalism. Although I believe the "buck stops" with the elders, I will also argue that Scripture portrays these elders as:

A. Being receptive to the input of their *local congregation*.

B. Being eager for meaningful input from *outside the local congregation*, such as one or two leaders/elders of other churches who are known and trusted by the local elders, maybe from within an association the church is part of.

C. Having a clear and empowered *first-among-equals* leader, who may be called the Lead Elder or Senior Pastor, although he is quite different from the CEO-style Senior Pastor customary in many churches today, and the team quite different from the "Executive Board" style of eldership that tends to accompany the CEO model. To the contrary, all the elders – whether staff or non-staff – would be practicing pastors in some way, and enjoy a brotherly and collaborative atmosphere on their team.

Without diminishing the weight of my convictions around these things, I appreciate that Scripture is not prescriptive on the details of how such plurality should work, and therefore some of my inferences should be held lightly, and we should be comfortable with a fairly broad range of acceptable practice.

PLURALITY

The Bible sometimes specifies and often implies that churches should be governed by a plurality of elders. For example:

- *The Jerusalem church* had a plurality of elders (Acts 11:30, 15:2). We know that this was a very large church, so we should not think that plurality of elders is only for small churches.

- In terms of the *first churches they planted*, Paul and Barnabas appointed "elders for them in every church" (Acts 14:23). The accent is on plurality, and "every" implies that this form of church government should be universal. These churches were likely small, so we should not think that plurality of elders is only for large churches.

- The *Cretan churches*, also likely small churches, had a plurality of elders (Titus 1:5). Note also how Paul instructs Titus to appoint "elders in *every* town," again implying the universality of this model.

- The *Ephesian church* had a plurality of elders (Acts 20:17, 1 Tim. 4:14).

- Churches in the Roman provinces of *Asia Minor* had a plurality of elders (1 Pet. 1:1-2, 5:1-2). Also, Peter wrote this epistle as a general letter to many different churches, again implying that plurality of elders was the universal model.

- The *multiple churches that received James' letter* had a plurality of elders (Jas. 1:1, 5:14). This, too, was a general letter to many different churches, implying that plurality of elders was the universal model.

- The *church that received the letter to the Hebrews* had a plurality of leaders, likely elders (Heb. 13:17).

- In 1 Timothy 3:2 and Titus 1:7, the singular word, "elder," is used. However, both the context and the Greek word used suggest this is a representative "singular" amongst a "plural."

- We may also argue inferentially from the *nature of the church*. Congregations are multi-membered, multi-gifted, inter-dependent bodies of believers (1 Cor. 12; Eph. 4). An autocratic one-man model of leadership would be inconsistent with this, whereas a multi-membered, multi-gifted, inter-dependent body of elders is thoroughly compatible.

When John introduced himself as "the elder" (singular) in 2 John and 3 John, he was likely referring to his old age rather than implying that he was the single elder in a local church. (Paul used the parallel Greek word in Philemon 9, when he referred to himself as an old man.)

Some point to Timothy, in Ephesus, as justification for a one-man model of leadership. However, as we have already said, both Acts 20:17 and 1 Timothy 4:14 infer a plurality of elders in Ephesus, and it is likely that Timothy was in Ephesus as a temporary apostolic delegate more than a lead elder.[12] A similar argument is sometimes presented for Epaphras, in Colossae, but this is equally tenuous. He was certainly the original evangelist or "church planter" (Col. 1:7, 4:12), but more than that we can only speculate.

We have to conclude that all New Testament churches, irrespective of size, location, ethnic make-up, or who planted them, were led by a plurality of elders. An army of respected Bible scholars concur:

- Alexander Strauch writes, "Church leadership is a team effort, not the sole responsibility of one "professional" religious leader."[13]

- Bruce Stabbert writes, "The seven clear passages which teach the existence of plural elders in single local assemblies … should be allowed to carry hermeneutical weight over the eight other plural passages that teach neither singularity nor plurality. This is a case where the clear passages must be permitted to set the interpretation for the obscure."[14]

- Jeramie Rinne has a whole chapter entitled *Shepherd Together*, and speaks of church leadership as a "team sport."[15] He analogizes an eldership team with a Swiss Army Pen

Knife, where each elder brings a different gift/s to the team.

Pragmatic *experience* also affirms the value of plurality. Eldership teams minimize the weaknesses and amplify the strengths of the individual members. Few burdens seem heavy when everyone lifts. Few enemies seem intimidating with brothers at your side. Few fortresses seem unassailable when you charge them together. Eldership teams have more resources, more wisdom, more energy and more fun than an individual working alone. They share the credit for victories and the blame for defeats, which fosters humility and minimizes pride among the team members. Rinne writes:

> When elders are practicing a healthy plurality, it's harder for one man's views or tendencies to dominate, because the elders offset one another. The gentle elders temper the more fiery ones. The activists move the analyzers towards actually making decisions. The big-faith elders keep every decision from being one more exercise in fiscal conservatism and risk management, while the practical elders help the dreamers and visionaries not do stupid things under the pretext of 'trusting God.'[16]

Sometimes a church finds itself in position where it has just one elder or no elders. This might be because it is a church plant and elders have not yet emerged, or because of a crisis that has removed the existing elders. In these situations, it is usually best for someone from the outside to play a "Titus on Crete" role to help appoint new elders. This role could be played by a trusted elder or eldership team from another church, or from the group to which the church affiliates.

AUTHORITY

Due to our human propensity to either abuse authority or rebel against it, "authority" has become a toxic word in many cultures. Yet, one cannot read Scripture without acknowledging that elders are entrusted with responsibility (which implies commensurate authority) to govern the local church in both *doctrinal* and *general* matters.

In terms of doctrinal matters, elders are called to teach the flock the word of God, give instruction in sound doctrine, and rebuke those who contradict it (1 Tim. 3:2, Titus 1:9, 1 Tim. 5:17). Paul charged Timothy (who was either an elder at Ephesus, or working as an apostolic delegate amongst the elders) to "keep a close watch on yourself and *on the teaching*" (1 Tim. 4:16). And it was "the apostles *and the elders*" who met to decide on certain doctrinal matters in Acts 15:3. Of course, this doesn't imply there should be passivity amongst the congregation in terms of doctrinal discernment. Like the Bereans, they should eagerly receive teaching from their elders as well as examine the Scriptures for themselves to see if what is being taught is correct (Acts 17:11). Neither does this imply that the congregation should be passive in terms of "teaching and admonishing one another in all wisdom" (Col. 3:16). A wise eldership team will cultivate a general culture of believer-to-believer encouragement and support, as well as equipping believers to teach and counsel one another in different contexts. But overseeing all of this are the elders, ultimately entrusted with responsibility for sound doctrine in the church.

In terms of governing general matters:

- The various names for elders (pastor, shepherd, overseer) imply broad governance.

- We read in 1 Timothy 5:17, "Let the elders who rule well be considered worthy of double honor, especially those who labor in preaching and teaching." This suggests that elders also "rule" the church in matters other than doctrine (preaching and teaching).

- 1 Timothy 3:4-5 tells us that part of an elder's authentication comes from "managing" his home well, as opposed to "ruling on doctrine in his home," also implying broad governing/managing responsibility in the church.

- In 1 Peter 5:1-4, Peter's exhortation to elders supposes a broad governing role, as does Paul's exhortation to the Ephesian elders in Acts 20:28.

- The warnings for elders to avoid being domineering further intimates they had broad governing powers (1 Peter 5:3).

- Assuming (as I do) that Hebrews 13:17 refers to elders, the exhortation for the congregation to submit to the elders indicates that elders govern in all matters arising within the church.

Some churches restrict the elders' influence to doctrinal and pastoral matters, and appoint another group, maybe a deacon board, to rule on general governance matters. I have the following concerns with this approach:

- As we have seen, it does not seem to be *biblical*.

- It seems *illogical* for a community of people to trust the elders with greater matters of doctrine but not lesser matters of governance. Of course, wise elders know they are not skilled in all areas, and will delegate responsibilities to suitably qualified others and be receptive to their recommendations, but the elders should retain overall governance.

- It seems "top-heavy" to have another executive team to act as a check-and-balance to a healthy team of elders that itself would include a diversity of gifting and perspective, and that is amenable to counsel from deacons and other respected members.

- Generally speaking, I have observed that churches whose elders only govern doctrinal matters tend to attract "bookish" elders who struggle to rally God's people to much more than showing up on a Sunday to listen to them teach sound doctrine. Elders should be both teachers *and* leaders, and should be authorized to lead the church in both doctrinal *and* general matters.

In all this, I am not suggesting that elders monopolize the day-to-day leadership and ministry of the church, a theme that I will return to in the next chapter.

REFLECTION

1. Elders today can trace their origins to both the Old and New Testaments, and remarkably, there will even be twenty-four elders in heaven. How does this impact the way you think about eldership?

2. What terminology does your church use for elders, and why? Do you feel your terminology both honors Scripture and serves your culture and context? Elaborate.

3. Have you had any experience with Episcopal or Presbyterian forms of polity? If so, what are your observations on their biblical viability, and their strengths and weaknesses?

4. Have you had any experience with the Congregational variations of the one-man model, the fully democratic model or the corporate model? If so, what are your observations on their biblical viability, and their strengths and weaknesses?

5. On a scale of 1 to 5 (with 5 being "very"), how convinced are you of the biblical evidence for eldership plurality? Briefly elaborate.

6. On a scale of 1 to 5 (with 5 being "very"), how comfortable are you with elders having authority over both doctrinal and general matters in the church? Elaborate.

CHAPTER 4

FATHERS AND MOTHERS

*The Church is a family, and it will only flourish to the
extent that we value, honour and esteem women and
men, mothers and fathers, sisters and brothers.*
– Andrew Wilson

Much has been written and said over the centuries and particularly in recent years about the roles of men and women in society, the home and the church. And there is much disagreement. Such is the importance and breadth of the topic, elders will need to do their own work and come to their own conclusions. To help them on their way, I will try to concisely express my views on the matter: in short, I do believe Scripture teaches us that, properly understood, eldership is a role that only men can fulfill.

In our cultural context, this is a tough one to swallow, but I think a lot of that comes down to our **confusion of categories**. Most significant is that in our modern, technologically shaped world, we are prone to think of people in mechanistic ways. This means that we tend to read the term 'elder' as meaning the same thing as 'leader' does in business, politics or industry. In those spheres, it makes sense for the person – irrespective of their sex – who is most competent to be given the position of CEO, president or manager. But when the Bible describes the role of elders it doesn't really have our **corporate** contemporary leadership models in view. Rather, the picture is far more of the church as a **family**, which is overseen and protected by fathers. These fathers are expected to have certain gifts (for example, being able to teach); but their primary qualification is their godly character as fathers. This is made especially clear in Paul's first letter to Timothy. Throughout this letter Paul relates the biological family to the family of the church, and the church family to the biological one. This is especially plain in his instruction that a man should only be recognized as an elder if he is a good father of his biological family. This is a point that cannot be emphasized enough: *elders must be fathers*. Normally that means they will have their own families. Always it must mean they are able to father the church.

All kinds of people (of both sexes) should lead in all kinds of areas of church life and ministry – but only men can be fathers. Women should not be elders because women cannot be fathers. This is not to say that a woman should not lead a business as the CEO or lead a nation as the President or Prime Minister, as those areas of life are not in the same category as a church *family*. And, as I will soon say, it does not mean that women should not hold extremely significant positions of leadership in the church.

If elders are fathers, and women cannot be fathers, then can unmarried men or married men without children be elders? I believe so. Being a spiritual father means two things: being a man and having a fatherly, spiritual demeanor. More about this in Chapter 22.

When eldership is understood in this fatherly sense, it is much easier to grasp what we mean when we talk about the *complementarity* of men and women. If there are fathers in the church then there must also be mothers, and sisters and brothers. When thinking about these things I work my way down a "funnel" of consideration, working from greater to lesser:

My first and broadest thought is the **symphony of creation**. Think of the harmonious pairings in creation: sun and moon, sea and sky, and heaven and earth. A basic building block of creation seems to be complementary pairs that are equal in worth although different in function. It is also worth noting that some societies throughout the ages have assigned sex distinctions to these aspects of creation: the sun is always masculine while the moon is feminine. The sea is 'she' while rocks are 'he.' Complementarity is woven into the very fabric of the universe.

Then my mind goes to similar **concordant pairings amongst humans**: father and mother, husband and wife, son and daughter, and brother and sister. In contrast to cultures that regard women as inferior to men, the Bible teaches that these pairs are fully equal in worth. They are equal beneficiaries of the divine image and earthly rule and equal recipients of the Holy Spirit and his gifts, and they have equal access to the blessings of salvation (Gen. 1:26-28, Acts 2:17-18, 1 Cor. 12:7, Gal. 3:28). Yet in contrast to cultures that blur, even erode distinctions between male and female, the Bible teaches that whilst equal, men and women have certain God-ordained differences in roles. For example, this syncs with our experience as a married couple: Ashleigh and I are physically and emotionally different from each other which enables us to be a harmonious and complementary pair in life. She can bear children, I cannot. She has a motherly bond with our sons that I cannot emulate. She has a perspective on life in our church that I do not. But I am better suited to bear the responsibility of protection, and I have a fatherly bond with our sons that Ashleigh cannot have, and I have a perspective on church life that Ashleigh does not. Our differences are not a source of antagonism but the foundation of our complementarity.

Progressing down the funnel, I think of **church as family**. In the Bible, the primary description of God is father (Matt. 6:9, Eph 3:14-15). Unsurprisingly, the derivative primary description of the Church is family, with family language and warm relationship part and parcel of church life (Matt. 12:49-50, 1 Cor. 4:17, 1 Tim. 5:1-2, 2 Tim. 1:2, 1 Jn. 3:14-18). This is very important. Church-as-family not only lays the axe to the root of consumer church (where people come to receive a service, and then leave), but it brings into play the importance of the complementary pairings of fathers and mothers and brothers and sisters in church life.

Next, I think of **the importance of father-elders in the church**. If men are not playing their role in the church, churches will be like single-parent families. Many men should be able to play a fatherly role in the church, but, as I said above, elders *must* play a fatherly role. Importantly, this is fundamentally a **servant** role. As husbands and fathers lay down their lives in their homes, so elders do in the church. As I said in Chapter 2, in seasons of persecution, it is the elders who are taken in for questioning and imprisoned first. In seasons of pandemics, it is the elders who are leading in visiting the sick, and therefore putting their own health at risk. Protecting and serving is what true fathers do.

Certainly, there seems to be a consistent *pattern of fatherly leadership* in the Bible: The Levites, the twelve apostles, and the New Testament local church elders were all male. There are exceptions of a queen and a female judge (2 Kings 11:1-20, Judg. 4-5), but these were in unusual circumstances and, as such, should not be regarded as normative. It is also significant to my mind that Jesus appointed only men to be apostles. Although apostles are not the same as elders, by appointing twelve men and no women to be apostles, Jesus established a principle that not all church offices are necessarily open to women. One objection to this is that the culture of the day didn't allow Jesus to choose women for these positions, but this impugns Jesus' integrity and courage, and is inconsistent with how Jesus readily took on other cultural norms of the day, such as healing on the Sabbath, speaking with a Samaritan woman, and eating with tax collectors and sinners. I also note the pattern of male leadership throughout church history. The consistent pattern through the centuries has been that the office of elder/pastor (or its equivalent) has been reserved for men. Although this does not demonstrate conclusively that such a position is biblically correct, it gives us reason to reflect seriously on the matter before declaring that the church has wrongly interpreted Scripture on this issue through the centuries.

And then there are the *apostle Paul's* writings about eldership. In 1 Timothy we are told an elder should be the "husband of one wife" (3:2). Some argue that this is not a definitive argument for male elders because in this era only men needed to be warned about marital unfaithfulness. However, 1 Timothy 5:9 delivers a similar sentiment about women, saying that a widow should only be enrolled if she has been "the wife of one husband." Others suggest that elders had to be male in this particular church but not in others, due to a specific problem with women heretics. However, the same requirement is found for elders on the island of Crete several hundred miles away (Titus 1:6). Paul also says that an elder should manage his own household well (1 Tim. 3:4). "Although there were some female heads of households such as Lydia (Acts 16:15), if there was a man present, it was customary for him to be head of the household. Combined with the injunction to be the husband of one wife, this is a very strong indication that Paul sees overseers as fathers."[17]

Next, I think about **the importance of mothers in the church**. Titus 2 gives spiritual mothers explicit marching orders, and Paul's efforts to be both fatherly and motherly towards the Thessalonians clearly point to the need for mothers in the church (1 Thess. 2:6-8, 11). If women are not decently represented in church life and leadership, the church will be like a single-parent family. However, for a church to enjoy the influence of mothers, women do not need to be elders, so long as elders genuinely understand the need for mothers, and are proactive in releasing women into the myriad of roles and responsibilities available to them. Which brings me to my next consideration.

I think about the **importance of empowering and releasing women generally**, not only "mothers." Saying that women should not be elders is saying they should not be *fathers*, not that they should not be leaders. Many male eldership teams are close to hopeless in this regard. Some are lazy or unimaginative, and a few are plain chauvinistic. Others have got distracted as they have tried to restore a healthy model of eldership to their churches. I can think of some eldership teams who have commendably transitioned their churches away from congregational or one-man models to healthier elder-led models. However, as the pendulum swung, the executive function of elders was over-stated and the rank and file were unwittingly disempowered. In the preceding chapter I talked about the role of elders in governing both spiritual and general matters, but this should not mean that they monopolize leadership in spiritual and general ministry. I will argue in Chapter 19 that elders should equip others – not as an optional extra, but as a core responsibility.

Some elderships wisely structure the meeting rhythms of the senior leadership of the church to keep the emphasis on empowering other men and women. For example, the Eldership Team might meet once or twice a month to deal with the things that only they should deal with, whilst another team (maybe called the 'Leadership Team' or 'Elders and Deacons') consisting of suitably gifted men and women might meet more regularly to execute the bulk of day-to-day church ministry. Such churches may have women heading up massive areas of ministry and responsibility, with loads of people (including many men) answering to them. Certainly, there are many legitimate ways for elders to meaningfully involve women in the leadership and ministry of the church and ensure a well-rounded family tone. In her book *Jesus, Justice and Gender Roles*, Kathy Keller writes:

> Women are encouraged to be active, verbal participants in the life of the church – teaching, exhorting, encouraging, and contributing in every way except in the office of elder … The verses that mandate this gender-based distinction are provided with armor against the charge that their stipulations are time- or situation-specific only … there is something that is being commanded to the church that we must find a way to obey. Dismissing, ignoring, or throwing one's hands up in despair of finding clarity are not options.[18]

Kathy Keller is provocative here, calling for elders to make room for women in every area of church life except those prescribed for elders. Convictions around male eldership should catalyze not paralyze elders in making space for women to express their gifts.

Specifically, I think about the importance of **women deacons**. The topic of deacons receives fuller treatment in Chapter 14, but if (as I shall argue) women can be deacons, then having women deacons goes a long way to ensuring women are meaningfully involved in church leadership. Elders and deacons are a concordant pairing in church life, both vital to a healthy and empowered church. Deacons/deaconesses need to have character traits similar to that of elders. They may have a defined role in leadership, or may have more of a general mandate. Either way, they are serious leaders, and publicly appointing women to be deacons is a powerful demonstration of healthy complementarity.

A particular area to consider is that of **teaching**. Paul makes it clear in Titus 2 that *women teaching women* is essential, but beyond that he seems to envisage two other categories of teaching.

The first category, and by far the weightiest, is teaching done by *qualified elders or similar* (Acts 6:4, Titus 1:9, 2:1, James 3:1, Heb. 5:12, 1 Tim. 3:2, and 4:11-16). As we shall see in Chapter 18, it is impossible to overstate the importance of this biblical charge to elders. Falling into this category is the famous 1 Timothy 2:12 where Paul says he does not permit a woman to "teach or exercise authority over a man." It is clear that Paul has in mind some important limitations on women teaching, and by earthing his argument in creation and the Fall, we assume such limitations are for every culture and generation.

The second category is teaching that is open to *the whole church*. It is the "one another" form of teaching (Col. 3:16) that will sometimes occur in a public setting (1 Cor. 14:23-26). In contrast to the first category of teaching, it seems to be open to all believers regardless of sex or leadership status. To illustrate from 1 Corinthians 14, if women are able to bring hymns, tongues, interpretations, and prophetic contributions of various sorts in a certain setting, then to be exegetically consistent shouldn't they also be able to bring a "lesson" (ESV) or "word of instruction" (NIV) in that same setting? However, Paul doesn't elaborate on what is meant by these, and how they might differ from teaching by elders.

So then, what differentiates elder-type teaching from everyone-type teaching, and what contexts are appropriate for each? These are important questions for responsible elders who want to neither stifle the voice of women nor ignore the biblical limitation on women teaching. Eldership teams need to work out what teaching contexts they believe are reserved for elders (or men) only, and then should confidently equip and release women, and other men, to all other arenas of ministry.

I hope that women's voices have been well heard in churches I have led over the years. We have had active women's ministries where women teach women, women leading certain types of mixed-sex Small Groups, women holding varied and significant staff and lay ministry positions in which they often oversee men, and women teaching seminars and workshops. Functionally, the day to day ministry of the church has been done by a leadership team consisting of men and women. Our Sunday meetings have women involved in helping host the meetings, leading worship (and I mean actually directing the congregation in worship as opposed to merely being a lead vocalist), leading in prayer, interviewing and being interviewed, giving testimonies, and bringing significant prophetic contributions and words of encouragement.

In terms of the actual Sunday sermon, I believe that the routine, authoritative public preaching of God's Word is the role of elders. Therefore, I and the other elders (and trainee elders) do the preaching. We occasionally have a woman contributing a section on a relevant theme within the sermon. To help train preachers and hear a diversity of voices, we sometimes have other people (men and women) bring 5-10 minute "lessons" from the Bible (1 Cor. 14:26) on Sundays.

In closing, I must add that I think it is appropriate for a woman, or a team of women, to lead churches in situations or seasons where male leadership is not an option. I am thinking, for example, of situations in rural Africa where due to urbanization there are virtually no men left in certain rural villages. Women might also lead emerging churches for a season in pioneering contexts where women are the primary evangelists.

REFLECTION

1. On a scale of 1 to 5 (with 5 being "very"), how convinced are you that elders should be men? Explain your position. What is your church's position on this matter?

2. Outside of eldership, do you think women are sufficiently encouraged, valued and released into ministry in your church?

3. What is your view on women teaching? In what contexts do women teach in your church, and why?

Elders

PART 2

RELATIONSHIPS WITH EACH OTHER

Elders

CHAPTER 5

HOW LEADERSHIP PLURALITY FEELS

Elders are joined by shared calling, compelling vision, similar beliefs and values, complementary gifts, and true friendship. They develop clearly defined goals for which they share ownership, and around which they hold themselves mutually accountable.

In Part 1 we made the case for a church being led by a plurality of elders. We turn now to how leadership plurality actually works, starting with how it *feels*. The scarcity of clear biblical examples and instruction about how eldership teams function leaves us with significant latitude in how eldership teams may express leadership plurality. However, we can glean something of the feel of leadership plurality from other places in the Bible where leadership plurality also appears to be in operation, such as in the Trinity, in David's army, and in the apostle Paul's "team."

THE TRINITY

The greatest example of leadership plurality is seen in the way our triune God has made himself known to us: the Father, Son and Holy Spirit are three distinct persons; each person is fully God; yet there is only one God. Although they are equal in deity, we see a difference in terms of order. For example, we are told that the Father has given Jesus the name above all names (Phil. 2:9), and yet Jesus remains in clear submission to the Father (Jn. 5:19). The Holy Spirit is "sent" by both the Father and Jesus (Jn. 14:24, 15:26) and yet is himself fully God (Gen. 1:2, Jn. 3:8), and is sometimes called the Spirit of Jesus (Acts 16:7). The members of the Trinity are undivided.

Drawing application for an eldership team, although a lead elder would provide the team with over-arching leadership, another elder may have "a higher name" in a certain area of church life. An elder particularly gifted in preaching might loom larger than the lead elder in that regard, or the leader might defer to an elder particularly gifted in administration when it comes to matters of process. However, these elders would want to express their authority in their particular areas of responsibility in a way that submits to the leader and the team. When eldership plurality is in operation, although there is no doubt who is the over-arching captain of the team, it sometimes appears that Tom is leading, sometimes that Dick is, sometimes that Harry is, and other times that they all are. Although it is something of a mind-bender, this is precisely where the power of leadership plurality lies – it dissects *hierarchy and democracy* to combine the best of *leader and team*.

DAVID'S ARMY

Another example of leadership plurality is found in 1 Chronicles 11. Similarly to the previous example, it is something of an enigma. For example, verses 24 and 25 read:

> Such were the exploits of Benaiah son of Jehoiada; he too was as famous as the three mighty men. He was held in greater honor than any of the Thirty, but he was not included among the Three. And David put him in charge of his bodyguard. (NIV)

Try expressing that on an org chart! First, note how these men *complemented rather than duplicated* each other. Although Benaiah was as famous as the Three he was not included among the Three. He was equal in "worth" yet played a different role. Applying this to eldership, although certain decisions and contexts require elders to be equally engaged, elders understand that although equally called, they will express their callings differently and in ways that *complement rather than duplicate* each other. Also, note how Benaiah had a *specialist role* of chief bodyguard. Whilst all elders will have some identical shared responsibilities, where possible it makes sense to deploy each man according to his special passions and gifts as they align with the needs of the church.

PAUL'S TEAM

Paul had a group of men who helped him serve various churches. He was clearly the leader of this "team," but similarly to the previous examples, he expressed his leadership in a way that respected the plurality of the "team" and harnessed the power of the team members. For example, when Paul asked Titus to visit the churches in Crete, we assume that Titus willingly agreed. But when Paul "strongly urged" Apollos to visit the Corinthians, Apollos refused (1 Cor. 16:12)! How would Paul, the team leader, handle this situation? Instead of pulling rank and insisting that Apollos obey, Paul respected that "it was not at all his will to come now." And, judging by Paul's comment about Apollos visiting "when he has opportunity," it appears that Apollos remained soft-hearted to Paul's leadership.

We get a further indication that Apollos was a "team man" when, on another occasion, we deduce that he checked with the brothers before embarking on a trip: When Apollos "wished to cross to Achaia, the brothers encouraged him.... When he arrived, he greatly helped those who through grace had believed" (Acts 18:27). This blend of *individual initiative*, coupled with *respect for the leader and team*, is inspiring and instructive for elders. We strive to be mighty men, with mighty convictions, with egos mightily subordinated to the Lord and to one another.

REFLECTION

1. Is it clear who is the leader of your eldership team? Elaborate.

2. Is it also clear that you are leading together? Elaborate. Do different elders "take the lead" in different contexts? Do you think that is healthy?

3. Try and think of at least one unique gifting or ability each of the elders on your team has, including yourself. Take a moment to thank God for equipping your team with complimentary gifts. Any brief thoughts on how to release each member more in their complimentary giftings?

4. As per the Paul-Apollos vignette, is your leader confident enough to "strongly urge," and are the team members confident enough to sometimes decline for good reason?

Elders

CHAPTER 6
THE FIVE-LEGGED TABLE

In view of their resources in Christ, eldership teams should be able to harness the power of individuality and togetherness better than any unit on earth. This is the "secret sauce" of successful eldership teams.

The challenge for any team is how to maximize both individuality and togetherness. We see this ideal everywhere, from the motto on the back of American coinage "*E Pluribus Unum*" (Out of Many, One), to *The Jungle Book* mantra, "The strength of the wolf is the pack. The strength of the pack is the wolf." In view of their resources in Christ (1 Pet. 1:3), eldership teams should be able to harness the power of *individuality and togetherness* better than any unit on earth. This is the "secret sauce" of successful eldership teams.

To this end, think of an eldership as a pentagonal, five-legged table, where stability and effectiveness comes from all five "legs" being upright, and being a similar length. The five legs are:

1. Individual   (each individual elder's role)

2. Leader   (the leader's role)

3. Team   (the team's collective role)

4. Outside counsel[19]   (the role of outside advisors)

5. God's sovereignty   (confidence that ultimately Christ is building his Church)

To harness the power of leadership plurality, no leg should be *regularly neglected* or *regularly dominant*, however, *different legs should be deferred to* in different situations.

NO LEG SHOULD BE REGULARLY NEGLECTED

If Leg 1 was regularly neglected (i.e. if some or all elders regularly lacked confidence in their own *individual calling* and conviction), individuals would not speak and act with conviction, and too many decisions would be abdicated to either the leader or outside counsel.

If Leg 2 was regularly neglected (i.e. if the elders regularly lacked confidence in the gifting and judgment of *the leader*), the team would get jammed up on decisions, go too slow, and lack cohesion and direction.

If Leg 3 was regularly neglected (i.e. if the elders regularly lacked confidence in the collective wisdom of *the team*), they would struggle to collaborate within the diverse perspectives on the team and make decisions that they could support in a unified way.

If Leg 4 was regularly neglected (i.e. if the elders regularly neglected *outside counsel*), at best they would limit themselves to the capacity of their team members, and at worst they would be susceptible to *group think*.[20] Because the nature of a blind spot is that you don't know you have one, a wise eldership team will invite trusted outside counselors in on a regular basis whether they feel they need particular help on something or not, and give them the freedom to raise any concern or idea with them at any time.

If Leg 5 was regularly neglected (i.e. if there was insufficient acknowledgment that the *Sovereign Lord* is at work in all circumstances), team life would develop a self-reliant, pressured tone. When things went well, pride would creep in, and when things went badly, there would be recrimination and shame.

NO LEG SHOULD BE REGULARLY DOMINANT

When Leg 1 regularly dominates, an *individual(s)* moves from a healthy conviction in his own perspective to being obstinate and "quarrelsome" (1 Tim. 3:3), and often holds the team to ransom.

When Leg 2 regularly dominates, *the leader* becomes overly assertive and suppresses the contributions of the individuals, the team as a whole, and outside counsel.

When Leg 3 regularly dominates, a healthy appreciation for *collective team wisdom* mutates into an *idolatry of plurality*. This can result in overuse of one-man-one-vote to make even small to medium-sized decisions on the team. (One-man-one-vote is occasionally useful for legal decisions requiring a record of a formal vote or to resolve a stand-off around a major issue, but overuse leads to all sorts of dysfunction including "analysis paralysis," stodgy decision-making, and "tall poppy syndrome"[21]).

When Leg 4 regularly dominates, *outside counsel* moves from the realm of invitation to imposition, intentionally or unintentionally usurping the God-given authority of the eldership team, and ending up weakening rather than strengthening the eldership team.

When Leg 5 regularly dominates, the doctrine of *God's sovereignty* is over-applied in a way that produces passivity rather than action, and abdication rather than responsibility. At best, such a team might be docile in decision-making, and at worst they might need the same rebuke that Joshua did: "Get up! Why have you fallen on your face?" (Josh. 7:10).

HOWEVER, DIFFERENT LEGS SHOULD BE DEFERRED TO IN DIFFERENT SITUATIONS

Deferring to Leg 1: Often the team will wisely defer to an *individual elder's conviction* on something. As a rule, in small to medium-sized decisions, deference should be given to the elder(s) carrying the particular responsibility, or with the most experience in that area, or with the highest level of faith for that particular thing.

Deferring to Leg 2: Due to his role and gifting, the *lead elder* is very often best positioned to make small to medium-sized decisions, and to be the primary architect of vision and strategy. Unless he is moving in a direction that is unbiblical, unconstitutional, or plain loopy, the team should eagerly follow his lead. A leader plays an invaluable role in helping the team avoid the "Ready, Aim, Aim," syndrome, just as the team guards against "Ready, Fire, Aim."

Deferring to Leg 3: For large to massive decisions, the majority opinion of the team should usually be followed. If an elder disagrees with the decision, his confidence in plurality and the *collective calling of the team* enable him to concede in good heart and back the decision of the team. Remember, unity does not equal uniformity. All are obliged to give their perspective as a decision is approached, and all are obliged to support it once made.

Deferring to Leg 4: Although the elders are the highest human authority in their local church and are therefore under no obligation to heed advice from elsewhere, they do well to be receptive to the advice of trusted outside counselors. Normally, elders would make the decision, however in crisis situations it can be wise to have a "parachute" clause in the church's Constitution or Bylaws giving two or three outside counselors official powers (e.g. a deciding vote) in the event of deadlock on the team over a massive or controversial issue.

Deferring to Leg 5: Sometimes the combined wisdom and action of Legs 1-4 will not be enough to resolve a problem. In such situations, the team should defer to "Leg 5" by restricting themselves to humble prayers to their sovereign Father: "We do not know what to do but our eyes are on you. Father, unless you build the house, we labor in vain. Build your church, Lord. Work this circumstance out according to the counsel of your will. Work this situation out for your glory and our good." (2 Chr. 20:12; Ps. 127:1; Matt. 16:18; Eph. 1:11; Rom. 8:28).

REFLECTION

1. Do you agree that all five "legs" contribute to healthy eldership? If you disagree with one, make a case why. Can you think of any other "legs" that are worth mentioning?

2. Is any "leg" on your team either regularly dominant or regularly neglected? If so, propose a remedy.

3. Mention some actual instances when your team has successfully deferred to different "legs."

4. Does your team have any official or unofficial "parachute plan" for crisis situations? If so, summarize it.

CHAPTER 7

ATTITUDES

Regulated by Jesus, elders know when to soothe and when to challenge, and when to press for progress and when to preserve the status quo.

Space does not permit me to elaborate on all the attitudes that contribute to successful plurality, but in my experience three stand out as amongst the most important: *conviction*, *brotherhood*, and *trust*.

CONVICTION

You will remember from the "five-legged table" analogy how important it is for each elder to have strong convictions about his own calling to eldership, that of his fellow elders, and that of the lead elder. Where lies the basis of such conviction, and what benefits accrue to a team with high levels of conviction in these areas?

The origin of an elder's confidence is foremost in Christ's headship of the church (Col. 1:18), and then in Christ's delegated authority to elders. Make no mistake, the risen Christ himself gives leaders to the church (Eph. 4:11-16) and the Holy Spirit makes a man an elder (Acts 20:28). Assuming a reasonable process of eldership apprenticeship and appointment, each elder may be convinced that God has called him and his brothers to lead their church together, and that God will give them the grace necessary to fulfill their mandate, including the promise of God-given wisdom (Jas. 1:5). Decent levels of conviction enable elders to:

- *Maintain motivation despite the mundane* aspects of eldership. Although they sometimes have to push through stodgy agendas, they never forget they are in the business of pushing back darkness. They are men bought by Jesus, called by Jesus, and equipped by Jesus, who boldly lead God's people into God's purposes.

- *Maintain their poise* in the disorienting days that we live in. They allow them to sometimes compromise on practice without ever conceding on principle.

- *Maintain flexibility in how they express their eldership.* Calling seldom changes but the way we express our calling often does. The Lord calls us to eldership, but our fellow elders help us express our eldership in a way that best serves the church and the eldership team in different seasons. And seasons do change in a church, meaning that the eldership team should adjust accordingly.

- *Collaborate around major decisions whilst delegating lesser decisions* to each other. To say it the other way, it is hard to collaborate with, and delegate to, men who you don't really think should be elders!

- *Be regulated by Jesus more than anything, or anyone, else.* Knowing Jesus has called them to eldership, their dominant thought is "what would Jesus do?" From here they find wisdom to know when to soothe and when to challenge, and when to press for progress and when to preserve the status quo. They are comfortable with adventure and uncertainty, yet sober-minded, steady, and committed for the long haul. They are both thick skinned and soft hearted, bounce back fast from disagreements, and readily overlook offenses.

BROTHERHOOD

I recently heard someone speculate that good friendships amongst elders might actually work against an effective eldership dynamic, because friendship can make it harder for elders to disagree with each other. Nonsense. Elders are mature men who know that speaking truth a loving way, in a loving environment, is God's best (Eph. 4:15), and that genuine relationship and a strong sense of brotherhood is mission-critical, not an optional extra.

The theological motivation for this is derived from who God is, and what God's church should be like. God himself is a loving, highly relational triune community (Lk. 3:22, Jn. 16:28) and the predominant description of God is "Father" (Matt. 6:9, Eph. 3:14-15). It is therefore no surprise that the New Testament church was a warm community (Acts 2:41, Eph. 3:14-15), with leaders regarding themselves as fathers (1 Cor. 4:15-16, 1 Thess. 2:6-8, 11-12), with family language and warm relationship being part and parcel of church life (Matt. 12:49-50, 1 Cor. 4:17, 1 Tim. 5:1-2, 2 Tim. 1:2, 1 Jn. 3:14-18). Therefore, elders who lead the *family* of God on behalf of their *heavenly Father* will want to truly be brothers.

There are also pragmatic reasons for brotherhood. Simply, effective and happy leadership plurality is impossible without meaningful relationship. Knowing and being known, and loving and being loved, enables high levels of trust and ownership. The better you know each other, the better you will be able to discern and promote each other's gifts. The better you will guard each other. Who would not want such a brotherhood? And, the congregation will notice your love for each other and imitate it. Eldership teams

74

that *feel corporate* produce churches that *feel corporate*. Eldership teams that feel *like family* produce churches that feel *like family*. Here are a few ways to enhance relationships on the team:

First, make sure everyone on the team is *theologically convinced* of the importance of brotherhood, and committed to the endeavor.

Second, grow the team at a *pace* that maintains decent relationships amongst the team. If necessary, limit (or even reduce) the size of the team to regain a healthy relational dynamic.

Third, be *vulnerable* with each other. Jeramie Rinne writes, "If you're an elder, take a risk and get real with the others. Don't be afraid to reveal your hurts and fears, struggles and sins."[22] This is excellent advice, but Rinne might be too gentle. I think it is less a case of, "Go on, take a risk and be vulnerable with your fellow elders," and more a case of, "Don't even think about becoming an elder if you are not willing to remain vulnerable!" Confessing struggles and sins to each other when necessary is not an optional extra for elders (Jas. 5:16). Vulnerability is vital if we are to build the strong bond that protects our team and our flock.

Fourth, commit to developing and maintaining relationships with each other *outside of meetings*. This can be done elder-to-elder or couple-to-couple through eating together, hanging out, even going away together. The more vulnerable you can be, the deeper and faster relationship will form. Not everyone needs to be best friends, but everyone needs to feel known and loved, and needs to trust each other.

Fifth, keep *elders' meetings* as relational as possible. Cultivate an atmosphere of fun, laughter and inoffensive banter. Build in some structured time when different elders share current highs and lows in their lives, and then pray for them. Any brother who is experiencing any sort of crisis receives unhurried attention. Remember, this kind of thing isn't a prelude to eldering, it is eldering (Acts 20:28, 1 Tim. 4:16). It is important for the lead elder to set an example of vulnerability and emotional warmth.

Sixth, *work smart and delegate well* to free up time and energy to build relationally. If the team is constantly over-worked, then brotherhood will take strain. Do not sacrifice relationship on the altar of task.

Seventh, *pray* a great deal together. Prayer is the most unifying team activity on earth.

Eighth, avoid *describing yourselves* in a way that tacitly undermines brotherhood. For example, if the concept of a "Board of Elders" conjures up non-relational corporate notions in your culture, then rather choose a more neutral description such as the "Eldership Team."

And finally, in the event of deadlock around a major issue or some significant breakdown in relationship on the team, *quickly invite in outside help.* Quickly. Not as a last resort. If you take too long you will likely incur way more relational damage on the team than if you invited someone in to help before the molehill became a mountain. Of course, the primary role of outside help is to help maximize the team's potential, not just to solve relational problems, but that is a part of it.

TRUST

Let us imagine the following "trust grid" analogous to the colors on a traffic light.[23]

Red	I do not trust you. You need to work to earn my trust.
Orange	I sort of trust you, and try to give you the benefit of the doubt. Prove me right.
Green	I trust you in a robust way, and my trust will not be easily eroded.

I once knew an eldership team who had several members on it who honestly thought that a culture of suspicion, particularly of the lead elder, was healthy. They had in mind how President Lincoln deliberately recruited a cabinet that was a "team of rivals." A cabinet of rivals might help unite a nation in civil war, but it will soon divide a local church. Of course, blind trust is not what we are talking about here, but in many ways trust is the life blood of an eldership team, and it can only be given and never demanded.

Given the importance of *trustworthiness in an elder* (see the characteristics in 1 Timothy 3, Titus 1, and 1 Peter 5), and given the *importance of faith* in the kingdom of God, elder-to-elder and elder-to-leader trust should be consistently green, with maybe occasional orange for brief periods, and never red. If it slips into orange, then immediate and thorough conversations need to be had to get back into the green. If it slips into the red, then the klaxon sounds, all tools are put down, and a solution must be found in short order. If you let it ride, things will deteriorate not improve. If a brisk return from red to green is not possible, then the only way to restore trust on the team will be by changing the team.

Trust is so important, that a church is better off with a smaller, less impressive eldership team who trust each other, than a large, impressive team who don't. Guard trust. Cultivate trust. Keep short accounts with each other. Keep no record of wrong. Ask rather than assume. Believe the best. Apologize quickly and thoroughly where you can, and stand your ground graciously where you can't. Disagree agreeably. Let no wound fester: clean it, bind it, and move forward in faith.

REFLECTION

1. On a scale of 1 to 5 (with 5 being "very"), how strong is your personal conviction around your calling to eldership? What might be eroding that conviction? What might enhance that conviction?

2. On a scale of 1 to 5 (with 5 being "very") how strong is the sense of brotherhood on your team? What things erode brotherhood? What things enhance it?

3. On a scale of 1 to 5 (with 5 being "very"), how strong is the level of trust on your team? Elaborate. Is there any orange or red in the mix? If so, outline a plan to return to green.

CHAPTER 8
ALIGNMENT

Do two walk together unless they have agreed to do so? – Amos 3:3 (NIV)

We turn now from key attitudes to key areas of alignment that enhance healthy leadership plurality. We will look at four: *agreement on key issues*, *size and composition of the team*, *effective elders' meetings*, and the benefits of an *annual check-in*.

AGREEMENT ON KEY ISSUES

Here are the areas I strongly urge elders to agree on before trying to journey together. It will require some hard work on the front end, but it will pay off.

Agree on the Vs

Agree on your vision. A vision statement reflects the unique sense of calling that your church has, which would no doubt be some kind of contextual re-articulation of the Great Commission. Agreement here will provide an invaluable grid to help the team know what to say "yes" and "no" to, keep the main thing the main thing, and guard against different elders' pet issues dominating.

Agree on your vital doctrines. An eldership team should have strong agreement around *primary doctrines*, broad agreement on *secondary doctrines*, and space for respected interpretations on *peripheral doctrines*. Without clarity here, major tensions and confusion are inevitable. We should be dogmatic where the Bible is, but not where the Bible isn't.

Agree on your values. Values speak to your philosophy of ministry, to the things you most value and most want to emphasize. There might be some overlap with "vital doctrines" but try to keep your values action oriented. For example, your top six values might be *Gospel Centered, Mission Driven, Word Honoring, Spirit Empowered, Prayer Fueled,* and *Discipleship Based.* A cluster of values such as these will serve as your team's true north.

Agree on your primary vehicles. Vehicles speak to your methodology, and the practical things that you prioritize to move the mission of your church forward. For example, your primary vehicles might minimally be *Sunday Meetings, Small Groups,* and *Serving Teams.*

Agree on a decision-making framework

Patient thought upfront in terms of who-does-what, who-needs-to-know-what, and who-gives-permission-for-what, will save you hours of time and stress as the size of the team grows. Think through what issues must come to *all elders,* or a *sub-group of elders,* or just the *lead elder,* or just *one elder.* Think through what things need the whole team's *permission,* what needs their *perspective,* and what things the team merely need to be *informed* about. Broadly speaking, I suggest entrusting *smaller matters* to the elder who has particular responsibility for that area, or the lead elder, or a combination of both. On *medium-sized matters,* the minority would usually be content to move forward in honor of the judgment of the majority, especially if the lead elder was part of the majority. On *momentous matters* (such as removal of the lead elder, or some key doctrinal dispute), unanimity should be pursued, and you probably need an official voting mechanism (with the help of outside advisors) to fall back on in case you cannot make a harmonious decision.

Agree on a framework to work through inter-team grievances

I suggest a simple Matthew 18-type approach to solving elder-on-elder disputes. *Step 1*: If you have a problem with a fellow elder, you should initiate conversation with him. Do not leave it to fester; talk to him and see if you can resolve it. Similarly, if you know or suspect that an elder has a problem with you, then you should also initiate as per Matthew 5:23-24. Similarly, if you are aware of a problem between two elders, urge them to obey Matthew 18 and Matthew 5:23-24. If they don't heed you, then you need to invoke Matthew 18 with them for that! *Step 2*: If the two of you can't resolve your issue, then draw in one or two other elders to help you. *Step 3*: If the matter still can't be resolved, draw in more, or all, of the elders, maybe with some outside help.

Agree on how to handle potentially controversial situations ahead of time

Two such areas spring to mind. First, *culturally controversial issues* such as sexuality and gender. Have an agreed position on these matters before you need them, or else you could be vulnerable if church members or the media suddenly engage with you around such issues. Second, *ministries that elders' wives or family are involved in*. If poorly handled (or even well-handled!), changes in these areas can cause friction amongst the elders. Imagine some worst-case scenarios, and talk through how everyone will need to respond if those scenarios ever occur. For example, imagine an elder's wife leads worship and both she and her husband think she is doing a great job, but another elder who oversees the Worship

Department views things differently! Wise is the team that talks through these sorts of scenarios before they need to.

Agree on how staff and non-staff elders work together

Communication, *capacity* and *personality* should be considered. In terms of *communication*, staff elders have little trouble staying "in the know," but special effort needs to be made to keep the non-staff elders abreast of salient matters. In terms of *capacity*, non-staff elders should all do *some* hands-on shepherding to avoid them becoming detached governors, but it needs to be recognized that their general output will be less than staff elders, and likely be in more specialist areas. In terms of *personality* type, non-staff elders need to be comfortable not being looped-in on everything, and delegating meaningful decision-making and implementing authority to the staff elders. I have noticed that men with a ravenous appetite for details and an unusually high sense of responsibility do not find it easy to be non-staff elders.

We look more at staff and non-staff elders in Chapter 15, but in larger churches thought needs to be given to how staff elders report to other staff elders for their staff roles. Clear but brotherly expectations and structures go a long way to protecting relationships and maximizing potential. Simultaneously being a lead elder, a brother elder and a staff "boss" to other elders is not easy, and thought should be given to how it all works. Try to think through who reports to who, how, and how often? What is each staff elder responsible for, and how is that measured? What recourse does either party have if the "staff" relationship is taking strain?

SIZE AND COMPOSITION OF THE TEAM

Size

Biblically, we know that an eldership team should be plural, meaning there should be at least two elders. If the church is small, it is easy to imagine just two or three elders, but what when a church grows? We know there is wisdom in a multitude of counselors (Prov. 15:22), so it follows that the more elders the more wisdom. However, because eldership is about more than men pooling their wisdom on various matters, there is a point of diminishing returns. In my experience, the dynamic of a team *always* changes as it grows, so every team will eventually hit a size where the compromises are not worth the benefits. The optimal size for a team depends on several tangible and intangible factors, so all I can do is mention a few of them in the hope that each team can apply them to their own situation to help them work out their optimal size.

First, and quite obviously, is the matter of *suitability*. If you only have two men who are biblically suitable to be elders, then that is your eldership team for now, no matter how big the church is. However, you can invite others to sit in with you and assist you until you are ready to appoint more elders.

Second, the team's *ability to delegate* genuine responsibility amongst themselves, and to others, is a factor. When levels of trust and ability to delegate are high, a team can usually be larger without compromising efficiency.

Third, *philosophy of pastoral care* is a factor. If the team believes that weighty pastoral responsibility should only be provided by duly appointed elders, then the eldership team will need to keep growing in proportion to the growth of the church. Or, if the team is comfortable to equip and release lay leaders to meaningful pastoral responsibility (reporting to the elders), then the team can remain smaller without limiting church growth.

Fourth, given it is generally true that it is easier to cultivate and maintain deeper *relationships* amongst a smaller team than a larger team, then a team with a higher value on relationship might choose to limit the size of their team to safeguard their relational value, or at least to grow at a slower pace.

Fifth, the *preference of the leader* is something to consider. The leader is the primary culture-shaper on the team and is held to account more than the other elders for team health and efficiency, so he obviously needs to have a major say in both the size and composition of the team.

Composition

It is not always wise or possible to appoint every man who could be an elder. Other than their personal suitability (character and competence) and their sense of calling, I consider five *other* things before appointing an elder:

Capacity: He might have great character, high charisma, and strong competency, but if he lacks the capacity to fulfill the demands on him as an elder in your church (maybe due to the demands of his family situation, or work, or health), then I would not make him an elder.

Context: If you are trying to grow an ethnically diverse church, you might need to refrain from appointing more and more elders from the dominant culture. It might be better to have a smaller eldership team that is proportionally more diverse. Similarly, it might not be wise to appoint men in their fifties and sixties in a church that desperately needs the next generation to take more ownership, or vice versa.

Chemistry: It is not good to have a cliquey team where everyone is best friends, but it is equally unwise to think that you can build a healthy team if there are oil-and-water personalities in the mix. Building a happy and effective team with compatible personalities is hard enough!

Balance of roles: Thinking ahead to the primary roles of elders in Part 5 (shepherd, teach, equip, lead), whilst all elders should have a basic proficiency in all four areas, ideally different individuals will be particularly gifted in *different* roles, and this will produce a well-rounded yet potent team. Therefore, it might not be wise to keep appointing teacher-types to a team that is already very strong in that department but lacking in the areas of pastoral care, equipping and out-and-out leadership.

Balance of strengths: I worked with one eldership team who had a personality strengths assessment done, and it emerged that of the sum of the elders, the percentage of the "go-getter" characteristic on the team was 7%, and that the leader contributed almost all of that 7%! I pointed out that this would create an adversarial relationship between the leader and the team, as he would have few allies for his progressive brand of leadership, and that the risk-averse team would unconsciously herd together and ostracize him. I hoped I wasn't right, but I was, and within a year the compounding friction caused a spark, and the team went up in flames. This was an extreme scenario, but it makes the point that a healthy and happy team is not just pot-luck, and that strengths profiles are something to consider.

EFFECTIVE MEETINGS

There are so many different ways to run successful meetings. I know some teams who have hardly any agenda or structure and who seem to laugh their way through copious cappuccinos, but who somehow stay happy and productive. I know other teams whose meetings are, well, at the other end of the spectrum, and also seem to be happy and fruitful. That said, here are my suggestions:

First, meet *frequently* enough to allow the team meeting to be not only efficient, but also to be relational. If the agenda is too tightly packed you will forfeit some important (often spontaneous) "off road" moments that build relationships, whether it simply be enough time to laugh together, or time to check in with a brother who is struggling.

Second, keep the meetings to a *length* that brings the best out of the team. When meetings regularly drag on, morale and productivity will wane, and the risk of unbrotherly behavior will increase. Be concise whenever possible. Remember that a good point will sell itself.

Third, ensure quality time for *prayer* either in the meetings, or in another regular context.

Fourth, *delegate* as much brainstorming and other prep work to sub-groups to maximize the efficiency of the meetings when the team are all together.

Fifth, try and give some regular time to the various *essential aspects of eldership* (shepherd, teach, equip, lead). You might do this intuitively or you might try to plan your agendas to ensure that over a six-month period decent time is spent on all categories to help produce a biblically balanced expression of eldership in your church.

Sixth, make sure that the *real debate doesn't begin after the meeting*. This is not to say that team members shouldn't process together in appropriate ways outside of meetings, but be careful that such behavior doesn't undermine meetings and make them empty rituals.

And finally, have a *capable facilitator*. Elders' meetings are so central to team life that the lead elder will normally want to lead the meetings, but he will often need a facilitator of some sort to help him ensure that the meetings are productive and healthy. Some lead elders are superb facilitators and can comfortably lead and "chair" their own meetings, but this is rare. I personally prefer to ask another suitably gifted elder to facilitate parts of our meetings to enable me contribute to the discussion rather than just facilitate it, and to make sure we don't stall when discussing a complex issue (which I am prone to doing). I particularly like him to host sections of the meeting that deal with financial or legal issues, as that is not my strong suit. However, I do not abdicate my role as primary culture setter and team leader to a "chairman." Of course, in some contexts churches have to have a Board of

Trustees with a Chairman who may not be the lead elder, but that is different from what I am talking about here.

ANNUAL CHECK-IN

A healthy team will keep short accounts with each other and raise concerns along the way. However, many teams find it helpful to also plan a "check-in" moment once a year or so. There are many ways to do this, and with a bit of trial and error, each team will figure out a way that works for them. Some will include their wives, others not. Some will do it conversationally, others in writing. Some will develop their own questions, whilst others may want to use the following *7-C Check-In* that I find helpful. No matter how you choose to do it, I recommend that all elders participate in the check-in, both staff and non-staff elders. Staff elders might also participate in a separate staff review that focuses on their paid employment, but reviewing all elders equally bolsters a sense of brotherhood and equality on the team.

Calling

Over the last year, would you say that your sense of calling to be an elder has increased, decreased, or maintained? If it has increased or decreased, briefly explain what has contributed to that.

Character

Of the characteristics mentioned in 1 Timothy 3:2-7 and Titus 1:5-8, which three do you currently feel strongest in, and which two do you currently feel weakest in? Who are you personally accountable to, and how does that accountability dynamic work?

Chemistry

On a scale of 1 to 5 (with 5 being "very good"), how is your relational chemistry with your fellow elders? What aspects of brotherhood are you most enjoying? Are you experiencing any friction? How could your team deepen their relational chemistry?

Culture

On a scale of 1 to 5 (with 5 being "very"), how comfortable are you with the culture of the eldership team and the church? Which aspects do you particularly like? Are there aspects that you are struggling with?

Competence

Although there is some overlap between the various aspects of eldering, we could say that elders *shepherd* God's flock (1 Pet. 5:2), *teach* God's word (Titus 1:9), *equip* God's people (Eph. 4:11-12), *lead/govern* zealously (Rom. 12:8, 1 Tim. 5:17, Heb. 13:17), and *model Christian character and leadership* (1 Tim. 3:2-7, Titus 1:5-8, 1 Pet. 5:1-4). Which three of these five roles do you feel strongest and weakest in?

Capacity

Are you expressing eldership and ministry in a manageable and sustainable way? Do you need to shed some responsibilities? Could you take on more responsibility?

Church

Mention three areas of church that you feel are going particularly well at the moment, and two areas where you would like to see improvement. What ideas do you have to improve these areas?

REFLECTION

1. In which areas of *agreement* is your team strong, and weak? Suggest practical steps to help find agreement in the areas of disagreement.

2. What are the benefits and challenges of the current *size and composition* of your team?

3. Where is your team strong in *running effective meetings*, and where is there room to improve? Suggest some improvements.

4. Do you have any type of *annual check-in*? If so, mention its strengths and weaknesses.

Elders

PART 3

RELATIONSHIPS WITH THE LEADER

Elders

CHAPTER 9

THE CASE FOR "FIRST AMONG EQUALS"

What team would not want the stimulation and courage of a gifted leader? What leader would not want the security and wisdom of a gifted team?

In the previous chapters we looked at various attitudes and actions that "oil the wheels" of plurality. We now turn to one of the most critical success factors for healthy plurality – a "*first among equals*" team leader. The term "first among equals" or "*primus inter pares*" is sometimes used in political and religious contexts when one is trying to communicate that the leader is afforded an extra measure of respect and influence by the team, whilst simultaneously remaining equal and accountable to the team in various ways. In antiquity, the leader of the Roman Senate was referred to as "*primus inter pares*," as was Constantine the Great. In more recent times, some political leaders have also referred to themselves in a self-deprecating way as "first among equals" as a form of respect for, and camaraderie with, their colleagues.[24]

Although the phrase "first among equals" is not used in the Bible, it is a useful idiom to describe the type of leadership that we deduce from Scripture is appropriate to eldership teams. If an eldership team consists of a plurality of "equal" elders (which I argued for in Chapter 3), and if that team should have a leader who is "first" (which I argue for below), then should he not be a "first among equals" kind of leader?

THE BIBLICAL CASE

I believe that the *first among equals* model is the most likely to enable a safe and stimulating leadership environment for a church, and more importantly, is a biblical model. Here is why I believe that:

The biblical norm is that biblical teams have leaders. By way of illustration, the examples of leadership plurality from Chapter 5 (the Trinity, David's army, and Paul's team) all involve a leader of some sort. Actually, leaders more than teams stand out across both the Old and New Testaments, therefore having a lead elder who leads the eldership team would be consistent with this general biblical pattern.

"Body theology" calls us to honor spiritual gifts, which would include the gift of leadership (Rom. 12:8). If a multi-gifted body of elders is the appropriate unit to lead a multi-gifted local church body, then it makes sense that part of the multi-giftedness within the elders would be a team leader especially gifted with the gift of leadership. It would be strange to honor all other gifts amongst the team except that of leadership.

The apostle Peter was clearly "first among equals" of the Twelve – he is mentioned first in the various lists of the apostles in the gospels, and in Luke 22:32 Jesus said to Peter, "strengthen your brothers." Bearing in mind the Twelve Apostles functioned for a time as the *de facto* eldership of the early church in Jerusalem church, we may assume Peter was also the leader of the Jerusalem church, an assumption amply supported by what we read in Acts 1:15, 2:14, much of Acts 3, 4, and 5, and Acts 15:7-11. Since the Jerusalem church had a leader, then we can assume other churches also should.

As the Book of Acts progresses, James seems to have seniority in the Jerusalem church. Acts 12:17 speaks of "James and … the brothers," and a similar dynamic is implied in 15:13 and 21:18. Whether or not he was lead elder *per se*, it seems the elders/church at Jerusalem afforded him special influence amongst them, which is consistent with the principle of a "first among equals" leader.

The apostle Paul assumed different elders would have different roles. 1 Timothy 5:17 refers to elders who both "rule well" and "preach and teach" and who are financially rewarded for their labors. Although there is no clear evidence Paul is referring here to a lead elder as such, the point is that Paul assumed different elders would have different roles and gifts, a principle consistent with the practice of having a lead elder. Actually, most lead elders tend to fit comfortably into the specific category that Paul mentions here, being suitable for the role precisely because they are gifted to both "rule well" (lead) and "preach and teach."

HOW HURT CAN DISTORT THE "DYNAMIC MIDDLE"

First among equals requires perseverance and maturity because we tend to naturally bias to the extremes of rebellion (no leader, thank you very much) or *domination* (shut up and do what I tell you). Our "first among equals" model allows for neither, and will press an eldership team to find the *dynamic middle* where the very best of leadership and the very best of team converge. Finding this dynamic middle should be a pleasant journey of discovery, but can be particularly taxing (or even elusive) for an individual or team that has been hurt in the past by either too strong a leader or too strong a team. If that has been your misfortune, I expect you will encounter three particular challenges:

First, you will struggle to know where this dynamic middle actually is. If you have been hurt by a leader, your "middle" will be further toward the "team" end of the spectrum than is healthy. Conversely, if you have been hurt by a team, your "middle" will be further toward the "leader" end of the spectrum than is healthy. You will need to allow others with experience to coach you on where the middle really is.

Second, you might struggle to grasp that the radical middle is a *band not an exact point. First among equals* is an attitude more than a system. It is kinetic not static. It has to be, because its genius is getting the best out of different individuals on the team in different contexts. Therefore, sometimes the dynamic middle will be to the left of center to defer more to the leader, and other times to the right to defer more to the team or to a particular team member. If you try and secure an immovable center point with all sorts of codifications and protocols, you will corrupt the soul of spirit-led plurality. Enjoying the full bandwidth of the dynamic middle requires trust in each other and trust in the Lord.

And third, you will likely find yourself longing for the "middle" for defensive more than offensive reasons. Your motive will be more to "keep the balance of power" rather than get the very best out of both leader and team. This is an unhealthy way of thinking, and you will likely drift towards being a policeman. Again, allow others to coach you on the great *potential* of first among equals, not just on how it protects from danger.

Understandably, it can be tricky to trust once you have been hurt, and it can be wise to take a season out of leading to give your soul a chance to recover. Remember, "hurt people tend to hurt people" so it is not wise to lead if you are still badly hurt. But don't stay out of the race long. Lean into the Lord, and into others again, and you will return stronger, humbler, wiser, and more tender than before – exactly the kind of qualities needed on "first among equals" eldership teams.

Friends, despite the challenges "first among equals" is worth it. Think of the apostle Peter: without him the team of apostles would have been weaker and more vulnerable; without them, Peter would have been weaker and more vulnerable. Without them, his impulsiveness could have been dangerous. Without him, they might have been overly cautious. But together they made a great team. Of course, over-elevating a leader leaves him vulnerable to pride and aloofness, but conversely, under-elevating him leaves the team vulnerable to mediocrity. The genius of "first among equals" is that it leverages the strengths of both team and leader. What team would not want the stimulation and courage of a gifted leader? What leader would not want the security and wisdom of a gifted team? A called and unified team of elders, led by a humble and courageous leader, mobilizing a gifted and energetic church body, is a phenomenal concoction for gospel advance.

REFLECTION

1. Do you find all five of the biblical rationales for "first among equals" compelling? If not, why not? Can you think of other biblical reasons to either support or undermine the argument?

2. In your own words describe what is meant by the "dynamic middle." What kind of experience have you had with leadership dynamics in the past, and how do you think this might be currently helping or hindering you?

CHAPTER 10

HOW "FIRST AMONG EQUALS" FEELS

It is first among equals not first against equals. In every happy and effective eldership I know, the leader is fighting for the team's influence, and the team are fighting for the leader's influence. Each tries to "out honor" the other.

IT DOES EXACTLY WHAT IT SAYS ON THE TIN

In 1994 a wood stain manufacturer called Ronseal ran a series of advertisements claiming their product did exactly what the information on the tin (can) claimed it would do. Since then "doing what it says on the tin" has become a vernacular phrase for "by name and by nature." "First among equals" leadership should feel like it sounds. All three words are vital: *first* and *among*, and *equals*.

First: The leader will be afforded a seniority and influence greater than the other elders by virtue of his gifting and position as leader. Although other elders on the team may express meaningful leadership in different areas themselves, and although the leader is ultimately accountable to the team, *there is no doubt who is leading the team*. The team heartily empowers the leader to lead them, and celebrates his spiritual gift of leadership. In that sense he is "first."

Among: However, the leader expresses his leadership from among the team rather over the team, leading as a brother more than an executive. Although he is free to press for what he wants, like Paul with Apollos, he is respectful and big-hearted when he doesn't get his way (1 Cor. 16:12).

Equals: The elders, leader included, are equal in worth before God, in their calling as elders, and in their shared responsibility for leading the church. However, within their equality they celebrate a diversity of expression in their gifts, experience, and talents (Matt. 25:14-30), and happily play different roles according to their individual strengths. Although equal in their calling as elders, how they outwork their calling will be different.

The following table speaks to the important balance of both "first" *and* "equals:"

Too much "first"	Too much "equals"	"First among equals"
The team is squashed	The leader is squashed	The team and leader flourish
Elders are cheerleaders	Elders are handbrakes	Elders are supportive yet wise
Lack of decision-making process	Hyper decision-making process	Healthy decision-making process
Too big a target on the leader's back	Everyone's baby is no one's baby	Shared responsibility
Hard to correct the leader	Hard to correct the team	Both open to correction
Leader dominates and team abdicates	Team dominates and leader abdicates	Strong leader and strong team

IT FEELS LIKE "SIDE-BY-SIDE, NEARLY"

We once took our elders and their families to the circus at the end of the year to thank them for their commitment. One act involved a man standing with his two feet on different horses as they cantered around the ring side-by-side. Although it looked like the horses were exactly side-by-side, the outside horse was actually marginally ahead. The outside horse was the "lead" horse, although the lead he was giving was subtle. To the crowd's delight, at various intervals the rider allowed each horse to surge about a yard head of the other one, making the rider do the splits. But he always brought the horses back to their default formation, side-by-side with the outside horse slightly ahead.

This is a helpful analogy for us. The default formation of the team and their leader should be generally side-by-side (equals) with the leader marginally ahead (first). However, in certain situations, one horse might pull ahead of the other. This is fine so long as the gap is not too large, and it is not for too long, and no one falls off! I can remember lots of instances and seasons where I *really* led as the leader, and seemed to have special grace from the Lord to be ahead of the team on various things. I also remember instances and seasons where different team members, or the team collectively, seemed to be ahead of me. But most of the time, it feels we are side-by-side, with me slightly ahead.

Because ultimate authority lies with the team not the leader, the team know they are within their rights to rein in the lead horse anytime. But they also know that if they do that too often, or with too much of a jolt, it will frustrate the leader and make him wonder why the team ever asked him to lead! Reciprocally, the leader knows that if he pulls too far ahead too often, it will frustrate the team and make them wonder why they ever asked him to lead! But when both parties are committed to honoring the other, "first" and "equals" harmonize beautifully.

IT FEELS LIKE "MUTUALLY DEFERENTIAL"

Sometimes I hear teams say that "the leader is the accelerator and the team is the brake." I am not a fan of this metaphor as it unhelpfully stereotypes the leader as the only go-getter and the other elders as risk-averse, which should not be the case. Also, it feels adversarial more than synergistic, implying that the leader and team are opposite forces playing opposite roles. Nonsense. It is first among equals not first against equals. In every happy and effective eldership team I know, the leader is fighting for the team's influence, and the team are fighting for the leader's influence. Each tries to "out honor" the other (Rom. 12:10).

I love hearing leaders say, "Brothers, as ready as I am to proceed on this, I am eager that we feel a collective "yes" before we move ahead. How do you feel about this idea? What am I missing?" I love hearing teams respond, "You didn't actually need to check in with us on this, but thanks for doing so. Let's do it!" Or, "We are grateful for your initiative and eager to move forward, but would you be open to the following caveats?" Honor produces honor. If you want your leader to acknowledge the team more, affirm him more. If you want your team to acknowledge you more as leader, acknowledge them more. Never fight for your own rights. Once both sides start doing that, so begins the death spiral. The "life spiral" happens when all players are looking upwards to Jesus, worshipping him, and trying to represent him in their relationships with each other. Happy is that band of brothers.

REFLECTION

1. Which line in the table especially caught your eye, and why? Can you think of other lines that could be added to the table?

2. Does "side-by-side, nearly" generally describe your team and your leader? Have you got any examples when either the leader or the team pulled ahead in some way? What did that look like?

3. In your own words explain what is meant by "mutually deferential." How is your team doing in that regard?

CHAPTER 11

KEY CONTRIBUTIONS FROM THE LEADER

There are few things that frustrate elders more than a timid leader, exasperate them more than a proud leader, and bless them more than a confident yet humble leader.

Here are some key contributions that the leader can make to help produce a healthy first among equals dynamic. I will speak directly to lead elders.

LEAD YOURSELF

The most difficult member of your team to lead will be you. I recommend you work on yourself in the following areas:

Be secure and satisfied in Jesus

This comes first. Unless you are ultimately secure and satisfied in Jesus, you will look for security and satisfaction in your church and your eldership team, and there is not a whisper of a chance that they can provide that for you. It's a fool's errand, and will inevitably cause you to slip into behaviors that will test your team. Your desire for success may cause you to drive them rather than guide them. Your desire for affirmation may cause you to appease them rather than lead them. Your pursuit of achievement may entice you away from your moral and theological center to whatever doctrine or method appears to be pragmatically successful, which will exasperate and disorient your elders as you lurch from one "great idea" to the next. So, brother, as they say on airplanes, first put on your own oxygen mask before helping others with theirs. Breathe in the grace of God deeply for yourself before helping others do the same.

Resist pedestalization like the plague

The Bible is clear that leaders are a necessary gift from the Lord, and should be honored and respected. However, leaders should not be put on pedestals. Your team members should not expect from you things that should only be expected from God. That is also a fool's errand. In fact, it is idolization, and whenever something created is elevated to something ultimate, after the euphoric rush of elevation always follows an excruciating fall. If they deify you, when you eventually disappoint them, they will vilify you. Of course, you are not ultimately responsible for their attitudes, but you can do things to help them keep Jesus on the pedestal rather than you. Be humble and authentic. Share your humanity with them. Confess sin and weakness to them. Boast about how the Lord graciously uses you even when you are a knucklehead. And most importantly, teach them to be ultimately secure and satisfied in Jesus themselves, so they are not tempted to seek that in you.

Be a man of two blends: confidence and humility, and faith and vision

Lead confidently yet humbly. There are few things that frustrate elders more than a timid leader, exasperate them more than a proud leader, and bless them more than a *confident yet humble* leader. In terms of faith and vison, vision without faith is hollow and faith without vision is aimless. Be catalytic and consistent in both areas. Keep finding fresh ways to articulate "The Big Why." Help them to own the vision for themselves. When you hear them remind you that "doing so-and-so is not actually in keeping with our vision" and that "we must trust God to fulfill what we believe he has promised to us" then you may break out the champagne – they have understood the vision and they are in faith for it!

LEAD STRONG AND LEAD TOGETHER

If you take *lead* out of *leadership* you get *er-ship*. What direction should we go in? "Er, not sure." What should our ministry emphasis be this year? "Er, good question." What is the Lord calling us to? "Er, don't know. Let's vote." Brother, you are called to lead, really lead. But lead together. Be a man of conviction and innovation, be proactive and inspiring, but lead from *within* the team rather than *over* the team. In your heart, *need* the team rather than *tolerate* the team. Think of yourself as "leading the team that leads the church" rather than as the "leader of the church."

When I was leading my first eldership team, I felt God speak to me when I was traveling on the London Underground. We were a young eldership team and still working at getting aligned on the important stuff, and although I didn't realize it, I was getting sloppy at keeping us moving together at a similar pace. If you have traveled on the London Underground, you will have heard the iconic address over the PA systems whenever people get on or off a train to make sure they don't fall between the platform and train: "Mind the gap." I felt God say to me "mind the gap emerging between you and your team." The gap can take different forms. It can be *relational, philosophical* or *doctrinal,* or to do with *gifting,* or simply about *general speed.*

The relational gap

You don't need to be best friends with everyone on the team, but you should be relationally connected with everyone, and ideally really good friends with one or more elders. In times of relational peace, rather than neglecting relationship building, try to deposit as much relational collateral as you can which you can then draw on in times of tension. In times of tension, move *towards* each other relationally, not apart. Do not let issues fester. A warning sign that the relational gap is too large is you thinking, "Leadership is lonely. My elders don't understand me." They may not understand you totally, but they probably understand you sufficiently. And if they don't, the answer is for you to help them understand you rather than withdraw from them. Don't become aloof from the normal fellowship dynamics of the eldership team. Be amongst your team and amongst the people. If a few people abuse their proximity to you, the answer is to coach them, not to withdraw to an ivory palace.

The philosophical and doctrinal gap

Pro-actively look for ways to enhance the philosophical and doctrinal harmony of the team. Attend conferences with other elders rather than alone. Read the same books at the same time. Talk through controversial doctrines and hot button issues together.

The gifting gap

In view of your stronger gifts in some areas, it is appropriate for there to be a gifting gap between you and the team in those areas, but the gap should not be too large. Keep the gap small by helping to develop other elders in those areas. Colin Baron writes,

> It is interesting to note how often Paul left a church and allowed leaders to come through, later going back to appoint elders. When you are not itinerant, you have to provide creative ways to provide space for men to emerge to stand alongside you … other team members must be given opportunities … to blossom in their own gifts.[25]

For example, if you monopolize the preaching, the church can become overly dependent on your preaching gift, and it can be harder and harder for other preachers to emerge. Or, if you are the only one bringing leadership energy to elders' meetings, the leadership gap will likely widen. Use different elders to present matters compatible with their areas of passion and gifting, both to the eldership team and to the congregation.

General speed

Two African proverbs need to be held in tension. The first is, "Go fast, go alone. Go far, go together." This is an exhortation for the leader to slow down to the pace of the team. The second is, "Speed of the leader, speed of the pack." This is an exhortation to the team to speed up to the pace of the leader. Both will need to happen to "mind the gap."

LEAD TOWARDS BALANCE

Build a balanced team

We have already begun to say that eldership involves several main roles: *shepherding* God's flock (1 Pet. 5:2), *teaching* God's word (Titus 1:9), *equipping* God's people (Eph. 4:11-12), *leading/ governing* zealously (Rom. 12:8, 1 Tim. 5:17, Heb. 13:17), and of course, *modeling Christian character and leadership* (1 Tim. 3:2-7, Titus 1:5-8, 1 Pet. 5:1-4). Keeping all five aspects in play is no small feat, and the leader plays a vital role in this. It may come naturally to you if you are a "jack of all trades," or be more of a challenge if you are personally strong in certain aspects and weak in others. Similarly, if your team consists of elders who are each naturally strong in the same aspect(s) of eldership, then you will feel the team vehicle always pulling to one side of the road, and you will need to keep a particularly tight grip on the wheel to ensure your team stays balanced on all aspects of eldering.

Part of building a balanced team is being a talent scout: You don't need to be *the most competent at everything*, but you need to be *competent at spotting and deploying competency* on your team (or heeding the advice of another elder who is stronger than you in that regard). Well-rounded teams consist of sharp-edged specialists, and you need to spot and sharpen those edges. One of the main reasons that teams plateau is because the members are not deployed according to their strengths. Delegating the right things to the right people enables the team to play to the level of the *most* gifted man in every area. Delegation should be clear but not overly detailed, as this honors the creativity and gifting of the delegate. Equip, empower and promote your team members.

LTVC

There are four things which, if all in play, make for a strong and safe church: *leader*, *team*, *vision*, and *congregation*. When someone joins a church, they usually do so because they immediately find one or two of these things particularly compelling. For example, maybe they like your (the *leader's*) preaching so much that they decide to join the church. But as the months go by, they gradually get to know various members of the eldership *team*, and increasingly catch the *vision* of the church, and along the way make some excellent friendships in the *congregation*. The hope is that by the end of their first year they are feeling meaningfully connected to you (the *leader*), the *team*, the *vision*, and the *congregation*. This is a strong and safe way to build a church. Therefore, try to lead in a way that helps the people feel equally joined to all four "aspects" of church. The more magnetic you are, the harder you might need to work at ensuring people are not overly connected to you and sufficiently connected to the vision, the eldership team and the congregation.

REFLECTION

1. All elders need to have their fundamental security and satisfaction in Jesus rather than in ministry or somewhere else. Where are you, or could you be, tempted to look for ultimate security and satisfaction other than Jesus?

2. Which of the potential "gaps" are smallest (healthiest) on your team? Are there any gaps that you feel are too wide, or in danger of widening? What could be done to "mind" these gaps?

3. In terms of a balanced team, which of the five aspects of eldership is your team collectively strongest in and weakest in? Does the "vehicle" pull to a certain side of the road?

4. In terms of a balanced church, do you think people in your church are generally well-connected to the leader, the vision, the eldership team and the church community? Elaborate.

Elders

CHAPTER 12

KEY CONTRIBUTIONS FROM THE TEAM

Paul thought of himself as both a father and fellow worker to Timothy (Phil. 2:22). This is helpful language for elders. You are both following your leader and are a fellow worker alongside him.

In addition to working with the leader in the areas mentioned in the previous chapter, here are several other things for the team to be mindful of:

"FOLLOW" AND "FELLOW"

Paul thought of himself as both a father and a fellow worker to Timothy (Phil. 2:22). This is helpful language for elders. You are both *following* your leader and are a *fellow* worker alongside him. Sometimes you will need to be especially deferent to his visionary burden and whisper in his ear, "Make the call, brother, we will follow." Other times you will need to remind him, "Brother, we are in this together as *fellow* workers. Can we discuss it some more?"

To bolster the "follow" dynamic, it is important to afford him authority commensurate with his responsibility as leader. Give him generous latitude to lead you within the bounds of Scripture and your agreed vision and values, and encourage him to confidently execute the vision, strategy, and day-to-day tactics of the church. And if he occasionally colors outside the lines, don't come down too hard on him. Part of his (much needed) gifting is to draw very close to the lines, and sometimes shift the lines a little, so if you want a catalytic leader you need to take the rough with the smooth.

To bolster the "fellow" dynamic, reassure him that you are owning the vision with him. Speak of "our vision" not "his vision." Don't let him be the only catalyst or the only voice of faith. Also, if there is relational strain developing, or if you feel he is off color, take the initiative and move *towards him*. This will mean a great deal to him and reassure him that you in it together as fellow workers. All of this will also position you well for when he needs correction.

FIGURE HIM OUT

Hebrews 13:17 speaks about the "advantage" of having cheerful leaders rather than "groaning" leaders. Tragically, the least joyful area of ministry for many church leaders is leading their eldership team. Literally, they groan more at the thought of an elders' meeting than any other aspect of church life. This. Should. Not. Be. To help your leader serve you with joy rather than groaning, you need to figure him out. He will be trying to do the same to you and trying to adjust his style to serve the team, but it is as important for the team to joyfully accommodate his preferences and style to get the full advantage out of him. Leaders will have certain quirks that are often an integral part of their flair, and a wise team will accommodate, even appreciate them for the prize of a leader operating in his gifting.

To help figure him out, you could ask the following questions:

What elements of eldership team life are particularly important to him? How can the team ensure that those particular things are fulfilled? For example, I highly value a buoyant prayer culture on our eldership team. If our prayer time is dozy, I get twitchy. Similarly, I highly value our times together as elders and wives, as I feel our camaraderie as couples is mission critical, so I feel uneasy if couples don't prioritize those times or don't organize baby-sitters and so on. I also highly value a culture of encouragement, so I get bleak if we jump straight to critique before celebrating the strengths of a proposal or an event that we are reflecting on. I am also particularly passionate about elders personally modeling our values. I whole-heartedly agree with Peter Drucker that culture eats strategy for breakfast. Therefore, I like our team to talk a great deal about culture and values, sometimes at the expense of getting through the agenda efficiently! I am grateful for a team who refrains from rolling their eyes when I get verbose about values!

How does he like to process, internally or externally? If he is an internal processor, how can you give him space without him becoming reclusive or the team feeling left out? If he is an external processor, are you prepared for him to say unfiltered things that he might not really mean, or appear to make decisions that he may need to "walk back" the next day? I am an external processor. Just yesterday an elder sent me an email asking why I had changed the plan on something we had discussed a few weeks ago. I thought we were just chatting and he thought we were forging a plan in stone!

How large is the intuitive component of his leadership? I think that a part of the spiritual gift of leadership is intuition, and that part should be respected. Think for a moment about another spiritual gift such as an evangelistic gift. Evangelists speak to unbelievers in a way that may sound rather average, and yet unbelievers respond in droves! The point is, spiritual gifts really are supernatural, and therefore it should not surprise us when someone with a leadership gift has something of a "sixth sense" for what direction to go in, especially in the absence of clear scriptural data or common sense on a particular issue. I often like to lean on empirical data and common sense, but sometimes I am unable to give coherent reasons for my thoughts on something, and resort to subjective phrases like, "I feel that …" or "I have a hunch that …" or "I have faith that if we do that …" It gets weird fast if too many decisions are based solely on intuition, but honoring intuition often leads to surprisingly positive results.

KEEP AN EYE ON THE CARICATURES

Here are few caricatures of dysfunctional eldership teams. I have intentionally hyperbolized, and I hope no team perfectly fits any one of these caricatures, but they are worth keeping an eye on to ensure you don't drift towards any of them:

The Sycophants: We simply cannot believe how lucky we are to have the fabulous lead elder that we have. We feel our main role as elders is to encourage him, and pick up the pieces after him. If people push-back on his ideas, we warn them not to touch the Lord's anointed. Loyally backing our leader is what eldership is all about!

The Mavericks: The more our fearless leader says "Charge," the happier we are! We believe eldership is about recognizing, raising up and releasing people into ministry, and if we do it recklessly, so be it – at least we won't die wondering!

The Bottle Necks: We have meetings to plan meetings, write position papers on how to write position papers, and form committees to form committees. Our leader spends so much time preparing perfectly worded proposals for us that, in the unlikely event of us approving the proposal, he lacks the energy to implement it.

The Jury: Our elders' meetings are quite like a court room really. We keep our poker faces on during the lead elder's presentations, then pick away at them until all the faith has been sucked out of the room, and then we vote.

Protectors of the Realm: We have the sacred responsibility to protect our church from our lead elder. He says he finds it rather suffocating that he is the only elder being kept accountable, but we find him more docile if he is in a constant state of mild asphyxiation.

REFLECTION

1. Is your relationship with your leader more "fellow" or "follow" or a healthy blend? Elaborate.

2. Have a go at answering each of the four questions about your leader.

3. Do any of the caricatures come close to describing your team? Elaborate.

PART 4

RELATIONSHIPS WITH THE CONGREGATION

Elders

CHAPTER 13
WITH THE CONGREGATION

*In the end, no ultimate cures, formulas, or
constitutional procedures for decision-making will
safeguard the church's peace and unity. Only humble,
wise, servant shepherds can lead the flock through
decisions and conflict in love, peace, and unity.
– Alexander Strauch.*

The elders and congregation are inter-dependent and mutually-honoring because they are all of the same body, and all parts of the body need to work together to attain maturity and effectiveness (1 Cor. 12, Eph. 4:16). This symbiotic relationship between elders and congregation creates an environment that is neither autocratic or democratic, where neither maverick leaders nor disinclined congregants can dominate, and where the best of both leadership and followership can be enjoyed by God's people.

MAKING DECISIONS

We saw in Chapter 3 how the Bible anticipates elders governing in both *spiritual* and *general* matters. Since the "buck stops" with the elders, there needs to be clarity that it is the elders who lead the congregation, not the other way around. Of course, in keeping with the symbiotic nature of their relationship with the congregation, the elders will sometimes involve the congregation in helping them make certain decisions, and may entrust the congregation (or certain groups within it) with significant responsibility in certain decisions and processes.

For example, in Acts 6 the apostles (functioning as the Jerusalem church elders/leaders) meaningfully involved the congregation in the process of identifying new leaders. However, the vignette culminates with the apostles (not the congregation) laying on hands to appoint the leaders that the congregation had recommended. Although they significantly involved the congregation, they did not abdicate their ultimate responsibility of appointment. I am not recommending that the specific protocols of Acts 6 be adopted as the standard way for appointing leaders or making decisions, rather commending the synergistic and good-spirited cooperation between the elders and congregation.

Another example is found in Acts 15 where the elders appear to draw in the congregation on a decision (this time a doctrinal issue) much later in the process than they did in Acts 6. We are told in Acts 15:6 that "the apostles and the elders were gathered together to consider this matter" – no mention yet of the congregation. But by verse 12 it appears "all the assembly" were involved, and by verse 22, "It seemed good to the apostles and the elders, *with the whole church*, to choose men from among them and send them to Antioch with Paul and Barnabas." Again, we see a dynamic whereby the leaders actually made the decision but worked hard to make it "with" the congregation.

Neither Acts 6 nor Acts 15 mentions congregational voting, nor does anywhere else in Scripture. However, a certain kind of "vote" can be a helpful way to *communicate* to the elders the sense of the congregation, but not to *control* them. The elders might say to themselves, "For this matter, we are trusting God for majority approval in the congregation," but that is quite different from *requiring* majority approval. Sometimes national or state laws require "the members" of organizations – ecclesiastical or otherwise – to vote on certain things, but these laws were not written with biblical governance in mind. With some thought it is usually possible to find a way to honor the laws of the land without compromising the authority of church elders.

What about when the elders and congregation disagree?

Although rare, it is possible that a situation may emerge where the elders want to press ahead with something that the *majority* of their people were not in favor of. In situations like this, assuming the elders were not violating Scripture, or the church Constitution or Bylaws, or the bounds of reasonable behavior, a godly congregation would remain sympathetic to their leadership, acknowledging that God has appointed these elders to lead them, which may sometimes mean leading them to a place they don't realize they need to go. However, in such situations they could expect the elders to act in a considered manner, drawing perspective from trusted leaders both inside and outside the congregation. They could expect the elders to give those who are struggling every possible assistance to gain faith for the venture. Alexander Strauch wisely concludes:

> In the end, no ultimate cures, formulas, or constitutional procedures for decision-making will safeguard the church's peace and unity. Only humble, wise, servant shepherds can lead the flock through decisions and conflict in love, peace, and unity. Both the elders and congregation play a vital role in this process, and neither should ever be down-played, overlooked, or elevated beyond the biblical design.[26]

HOW SHOULD ELDERS LEAD?

The entire book is trying to answer this question in the greatest sense, so I will just mention here a few things that warrant special emphasis, or are not explicitly said elsewhere in the book.

From amongst the people

The elders in Acts 16 made the decision "with" the church (Acts 16:2), and Paul writes to the saints "with" the elders and deacons in Philippi (Phil. 1:1). Leading from within the congregation means leading with a "with" spirit rather than an "over" spirit. The spirit of "with" remembers that all believers are royal priests equally enjoying direct access to the Father through Jesus Christ (1 Pet. 2:9, Eph. 3:11-12). It remembers that although there are different God-given roles of service and leadership within the Body, all believers are fundamentally equal in Christ (1 Cor. 12:12-31, Eph. 4:4-6). "In the local church there are no rulers who sit above or subjects who stand below. All are equal brethren. However, there are leaders and followers in a horizontal relationship."[27] Therefore, elders will lead confidently, yet they will lead from *amongst* the people more than over the people.

Through the word and the Spirit

The Bible is the ultimate foundation of the universal church, and as such the elders should ensure it actively informs every decision, direction and emphasis of the church. Particularly, elders express their leadership by diligently teaching the people the word of God, refuting heresy, and protecting the church from false teachers (1 Tim. 3:2, Titus 1:9, 1 Tim. 5:17).

However, anyone who has been in church leadership for more than a few days will know that there is a perennial stream of decisions that the Bible doesn't speak to directly or indirectly. For such decisions, we should draw on the guidance of the Holy Spirit, experience, and common sense. For example, in Acts 16:6-10 the Holy Spirit actively directed where the next church plant shouldn't and should be. Similarly, in Acts 13:2, "the Holy Spirit said, 'Set apart for me Barnabas and Saul for the work to which I have called them.'" Therefore, elders will also actively listen for the leading of the Holy Spirit in areas that the Bible doesn't explicitly speak to. Personally speaking, occasionally myself or one of the elders will get a picture or dream from the Holy Spirit that will inform a decision, but more commonly I find the Spirit causes us to internally lean in a certain direction. If we don't feel a particularly leaning inside of us for an important decision, we try to give the decision more time and ask the Lord to give us "faith" or "peace" about the direction we should go in.

Through guarding, guiding and governing

Elders *guard* the church from heresy (Titus 1:9), from dangerous people or "wolves" (Acts 20:29), and through enacting church discipline when necessary (Matt. 16:16-19, 18:15-21, 1 Cor. 5:1-5, 2 Cor. 2:6, Gal. 6:1, Eph. 5:11, 1 Thess. 5:14, 2 Thess. 3:6-15, 1 Tim. 5:19-21, 2 Tim. 3:5, Titus 3:9-11). Elders *guide* and *govern* the affairs of the church by setting the vision and strategy, the pace and priorities, by appointing leaders, and by overseeing the raising and spending of funds. Despite their clear mandate to govern the church, they should steer well clear of over-shepherding the details of the individual lives of the people, and should respect individual conscience in extra-biblical matters. In Chapter 17 we will dig in to how elders are also called to "guard themselves" (Acts 20:28, 1 Tim. 4:16), an important aspect of healthy leadership.

Through appointing deacons and other leaders

Appointing deacons and other leaders is a significant way that elders express their leadership, because choosing the right people for the right tasks blesses the church, and choosing the wrong people for the wrong tasks doesn't! Choosing correctly is best done by trying to match people's character and giftings with the positions that need to be filled. Generally speaking, smaller roles can be filled by those with less developed character and who are less gifted, whereas larger and more weighty leadership positions require greater character and greater gifting. We talk more about this in the next chapter about deacons, and in the final two chapters about apprenticing and appointing more elders.

Joyfully, yet in the fear of the Lord

Hebrews 13:17 says that pastoral leaders watch over souls as those who will have to give an account. 1 Timothy 5:19-20 anticipates elders will be scrutinized and even publicly rebuked for certain failings. James 3:1 warns that teachers will be judged with greater strictness. I recently had a conversation with a potential elder who felt he might well be called to eldership but was hesitant to become an elder in view of being judged with greater strictness. I pointed out that if God was calling him to be an elder and he resisted, then God might judge him for that too – so he might as well be judged for being an elder than for not being one! But seriously, these three passages of Scripture provoke a healthy fear of the Lord in elders, but this fear is a joyful and confident fear because we are fully confident in God's grace, and that God equips and sustains those he calls. He knows that we are not perfect and will not lead perfectly, but He will see us through.

HOW SHOULD CONGREGATIONS FOLLOW?

Much could be said about this, but I would summarize the Bible's teaching about how the congregation should follow their elders under three headings: *intelligently*, *actively*, and *generously*.

Intelligently

The Bible expects congregations to submit to and honor their leaders (Heb. 13:17), therefore it is only fair that elders help them understand what eldership is all about so that they can do so intelligently, cheerfully and with a clear conscience. Given that elder-led church is neither autocratic nor democratic, it is somewhat counter-cultural and counter-intuitive, and definitely requires explanation. To this end, I would suggest teaching into biblical eldership during the membership process.

Actively

Blessed is the eldership team whose challenge is how to steer pro-active members rather than stimulate lethargic members. To start with, congregants should participate in the process of *appointing new elders*. This would involve getting to know new candidates, setting them in place with genuine faith, and charging them to enthusiastically shepherd them into the purposes of God. Second, the congregation should actively pray for their elders (1 Thess. 5:25, Heb. 13:18). Third, they should actively absorb the elders' teaching from God's word (Heb. 13:7, 1 Tim. 5:17). Fourth, they should actively imitate their elders' *way of life and faith* (Heb. 13:7). And fifth, they should actively *submit* to them "for they are keeping watch over your souls, as those who will have to give an account" (Heb. 13:17). Keeping watch over souls, and ultimately giving an account to God for that, is no small thing. It is what makes the job unlike any other. Strauch reminds us,

> It is all too easy to forget that the elders are Christ's under-shepherds. God has given them the solemn responsibility to shepherd his flock (1 Peter 5:1-4) and will hold them accountable for that responsibility. Spiritually minded Christians will not only submit, but will earnestly seek to be led by those God has placed in leadership.[28]

Generously

1 Timothy 5:17-19 mentions two areas in which congregants should be generous towards their elders. The first concerns

remuneration. The exact meaning of "double honor" is not clear, but it sounds generous! Maybe Paul used the word "double" because he anticipated the natural temptation to set staff elders' salaries too low. Hard work, especially of this nature, should receive generous financial reward, and those who have the responsibility to set church salaries should heed these verses.

The second concerns *generosity of heart concerning accusations or criticisms* against elders. A charge against an elder should only be considered if it is substantiated by two to three credible people. Although a rare occurrence, sometimes people will bring accusations against an elder(s). Sometimes this will be warranted, and other times not. Therefore, it is important to have a process in place that both protects the person bringing the accusation, and also protects the elder, enabling the charge to be considered (and maybe dismissed) with minimal pain to all concerned. Therefore, a responsible eldership team will coach their congregation about how to go about that process as and when required.

REFLECTION

1. In your own words describe why and how the relationship between the elders and the congregation should be symbiotic.

2. How are major decisions made in your church?

3. In terms of how elders should lead, which of the ways mentioned is your eldership team strongest and weakest

in? What steps could be taken to improve in the area of weakness?

4. In terms of how the congregation should follow, which of the ways mentioned is your church strongest and weakest in? What steps could be taken to improve in the area of weakness?

Elders

CHAPTER 14
WITH DEACONS

Elders are servant leaders and deacons are leading servants. – Church at Brook Hills, Alabama

Elders and deacons are the two "named" local church leadership groups in the New Testament. It is important to be as clear as possible on the role of each, for confusion in one can promote confusion in the other. In some churches, deacons are non-existent either in name or, more seriously, in practice, often meaning that the elders do way too much. Of course, there may not be a need for deacons in a small church, but the absence of deacons (or their equivalent) in a larger church is often a bottleneck to effective ministry.

The word "deacon" comes from the Greek word, *diakonos*, meaning "servant." It is used nearly thirty times in the New Testament, and in most instances, it is used in a non-technical, generic way. For example, in Mark 10:43, Jesus says whoever would be great among you must be your "servant." In Romans 13:4, Paul says civic rulers are God's "servants." But in Philippians 1:1 and 1 Timothy 3:8-13 the word is translated in a more technical way as "deacon" rather than "servant," denoting an office in the church, further endorsed by the fact that it is mentioned in both places alongside elders.

Although many assume that the seven men appointed in Acts 6 were the first deacons, there is no clear case to be made for this, as the word *diakonos* is used here in the non-technical way, and Luke later describes Philip as "one of the seven" not as "one of the deacons" (Acts 21:8). However, the appointment of the seven can be considered a *helpful prototype* for how elders can appoint people to the office of deacon or to other leadership positions. The first we hear of deacons proper is in Philippians 1 and 1 Timothy 3, so we assume that as the gospel spread and churches were planted, local elders mimicked the happenings of Acts 6 and appointed deacons to assist them in their churches. Certainly, by the time

Paul wrote Philippians 1 and 1 Timothy 3 deacons were regarded as an office in the church.

SIMILAR TO AND DIFFERENT FROM ELDERS

In terms of similarities to elders, the Bible refers to deacons as plural (i.e. more than one of them working in a church), and allows for both married and single deacons. There is also considerable overlap of characteristics:

> Deacons likewise must be dignified, not double-tongued, not addicted to much wine, not greedy for dishonest gain. They must hold the mystery of the faith with a clear conscience. And let them also be tested first; then let them serve as deacons if they prove themselves blameless. Their wives likewise must be dignified, not slanderers, but sober-minded, faithful in all things. Let deacons each be the husband of one wife, managing their children and their own households well. For those who serve well as deacons gain a good standing for themselves and also great confidence in the faith that is in Christ Jesus (1 Tim. 3:8-13).

Whilst generally irreproachable and dignified, and specifically principled in the areas of speech, alcohol, finance, and home life, deacons "must hold the mystery of the faith with a clear conscience," implying that they should be spiritually weighty individuals and orthodox in their beliefs. Verse 11 also says that their wives should be "dignified, not slanderers, but sober-minded, faithful in all things," a verse I will return to below when we talk about women deacons.

Deacons seem to differ from elders in that they are not required to be able to *teach* God's word and refute heresy like elders should (1 Tim. 3:2, Titus 1:9), nor do they *govern* the church like elders do. Whilst they will need delegated authority from the elders to fulfill their responsibilities, the biblical emphasis is on deacons *serving* not *ruling*. We could say that elders are servant leaders and deacons are leading servants.[29] There seems no doubt that deacons are subject to, and in support of, elders because:

- There is *greater emphasis* on elders than deacons in Scripture. Deacons are only mentioned in Philippians 1:1 and 1 Timothy 3:8-12.

- Elders are consistently mentioned *before* deacons, implying that elders have greater authority (Phil. 1:1, 1 Tim. 3:1-13).

- Their different *job descriptions* state that elders, rather than deacons, have the responsibility to govern (Acts 20:28, 1 Tim. 3:1, 5:17).

- The word *elder* means an *overseeing pastor*, and the word *deacon* simply means *servant*.

But make no mistake, "deacon" is an important role, and deacons receive an unusual confidence in their faith through their serving activities (1 Tim. 3:13), and set an example of Christ-like service for all believers (Mk. 10:43-45).

WHAT DEACONS DO

Scripture is clear that deacons serve in the church, but vague on the specifics of what that looks like. We may assume this vagueness is intentional, meaning that elders have great flexibility in how they deploy deacons. Although not deacons *per se*, the seven leaders appointed in Acts 6 were specifically appointed to organize the distribution of welfare, and, to ensure the elders were freed up to prioritize their primary responsibilities of prayer and ministry of the word. Mindful of this, many churches deploy deacons in more "practical" areas of ministry which seems to make good sense, although it is not wrong to deploy deacons in more "spiritual/pastoral" positions.

In our church, deacons play a three-fold role. First, they *bear some kind of organizational load*. Some lead certain key ministries, whilst others are available to pick up ad hoc responsibilities as required for a season. Second, deacons are *culture-carriers*. They propagate the values of our church. They also have spiritual weight and add spiritual ballast and maturity to our church. Third, deacons help the elders with *perspective and encouragement*. Due to the gifts and passions of the individuals concerned, and the seasonal needs of the church, some deacons may operate more in one category(s) than others. That is healthy.

CAN WOMEN BE DEACONS?

There are two passages that we can look at in this regard. The first is Romans 16:1 concerning "our sister Phoebe, a servant of the church at Cenchreae." Amongst others, John Stott, Douglas

Moo, and Leon Morris struggle to decide whether Phoebe is a servant in the general sense, or whether she served in the office of a deacon.[30] To my mind, she held the office of deacon because the word translated "servant" is the same word translated "deacon" in Philippians 1:1 and 1 Timothy 3 where there seems no doubt that deacon was an actual office. Also, Paul's stipulation "of the church" suggests that Phoebe was serving this particular church at Cenchreae in something of an official manner more than a general manner.

The second passage is 1 Timothy 3:8-12. The challenge is working out whether the women mentioned here are wives of deacons, women who assist male deacons, or women deacons, or a combination of these. Much has been written both for and against each option, and respected scholars disagree.[31] Stott summarizes both sides of the argument. His argument in favor of deaconesses is: "the 'likewise' of verse 11, like that of verse 8, leads one to expect a new category; it would be strange for deacons' wives to be mentioned when elders' wives are not ... and we know from Phoebe that there were women deacons or deaconesses at that time."[32]

I find this persuasive, but I conclude along with various commentators that v. 11 could refer to *both* women deacons and wives of deacons. In our church, this functionally means that whether we are appointing a married man or married woman to be a deacon, we must be satisfied that both they and their spouse are "dignified, not slanderers, but sober-minded, faithful in all things." (And obviously, a single deacon should also exhibit these characteristics). This approach not only "covers" both possible interpretations of this verse, but reflects our hope that spouses would be "together on mission," emotionally supporting and often practically assisting one another in their respective ministries, and also protects us from the slippery slope of explicitly forbidding what the Bible explicitly does not.

WHERE TO DRAW THE LINE

One of the practical challenges faced when appointing deacons is to work out where "the line" is between deacons and other leaders. For the sake of organizational clarity, many eldership teams decide to match people with deacon-like characteristics to specific positions of leadership in the church, typically of a certain tier. This approach may mean that not everyone with deacon-type characteristics will be made a deacon (because there might not be enough deacon positions for all of them), and it would mean that if a deacon stopped performing a deacon role, then under normal circumstances he would stop being a deacon. Other eldership terms choose to appoint people with deacon-like characteristics to the office of deacon without coupling that appointment to a specific role, deploying them to various roles as necessary. Whichever approach is taken, it is important that deacons actually serve the current needs of the church, and that expectations are clear. To this end, most churches I know appoint deacons for a term of one or two years.

REFLECTION

1. Does your church have deacons? If not, why not? If so, how do you deploy them?

2. Do you have women deacons? If not, why not?

CHAPTER 15
WITH STAFF

There are unique strains to your church being both your family and your employer. Therefore, church staff need particular care and appreciation.

GENERAL STAFF

I am using the word *staff* to refer to anyone who is remunerated by the church on either a *full time* or *part time* basis. As per this definition, the closest the New Testament seems to get to mentioning staff is in 1 Timothy 5:17-18 where it describes elders being remunerated for their ministry, and 1 Corinthians 9:14 where we learn that "those who proclaim the gospel should get their living by the gospel." However, it isn't necessary to make a direct biblical case for church staff any more than it is to make one for other key roles in modern-day churches that are not mentioned in the Bible. That said, the Bible is explicit about elders and deacons in a way that it isn't about church staff, and therefore it is important to think carefully about how staff "fit" into the primary leadership construct of elders and deacons.

To say it another way, I have noticed that staff who feel meaningfully connected to the primary leadership structure of elders and deacons (as opposed to a separate specialist unit) tend to be happier and more secure. Of course, the staff *are* a "specialist unit" in that they work together day-to-day, require their own staff policies and procedures, and need their own staff meetings and so on. However, if their specialist identity is overstated, they tend to either develop an inferiority complex ("we just do the grunt work") or a sense of entitlement ("we are the most capable and available") and can end up running the church as the lead elder's private army! There are several ways to avoid these two pathologies developing:

First, hire *capable and secure* people and ensure they are capably managed. Incompetent staff managers and staff will frustrate themselves and everyone else and place strain on relationships, and insecure staffers will be especially prone to either feeling inferior or entitled.

Second, *appreciate* the staff, because there are unique strains to thinking of your church as both your family and your employer, and your pastor(s) as both your pastor and your boss.

Third, *empower* the staff. Once direction has been set, empower the staff to make as many decisions as possible without having to revert to leadership for permission.

Fourth, help staff think of themselves as those who *empower and equip* the congregation, as per the Ephesians 4 principle of equipping the saints to do the work of the ministry. Staff can indirectly empower by diligently doing some specialist tasks themselves so the congregation doesn't have to (e.g. much of the basic admin), and elders can directly empower staff by making sure they don't play roles that should be played by people in the congregation; it is all too easy to "get the staff to do it" because they are available, instead of taking the time to meaningfully delegate to the congregation.

And fifth, *structurally* connect the staff with the elders and deacons. This doesn't mean that all the staff necessarily need to be elders or deacons, but if some of them are then why not call them "full time elders" or "full time deacons" to minimize the psychological and structural gap between the staff and the primary leadership units?

Also, staff who are not deacons or elders need to understand that what they are doing is specifically enabling elders and deacons to do the work of the ministry, which helpfully anchors their identity within those two entities. These five things grow in importance as a church staff grows and a church becomes more complex.

STAFF ELDERS

Thinking specifically about staff elders, assuming you believe in elder plurality and authority as per this book, then whilst staff elders might *function differently* from non-staff elders in terms of expressing their eldership day-to-day, they are *fundamentally equal* to non-staff elders in terms of their office of elder. The worth and equality of an elder should not depend on whether or not he is remunerated by the church or whether he does more or less "elder work" than his fellow elders.

It is therefore helpful to have a fire-break in our minds as we think about an elder's *office of elder* and his *staff role*. The fire-break is easy to imagine if the elder's role on the church staff doesn't involve any elder-type work, for example he might be employed exclusively as the church finance director, or as the caretaker of the church property. But the fire-break is harder to imagine if he is employed by the church to do mostly elder-type work, such as teaching, coaching leaders, evangelism, counseling and so on. In this situation, I am not suggesting the elder-type work that he does "on the church's dime" is either superior or inferior to that of a non-staff elder, rather that he is employed to *do* elder work as opposed to being employed to *be* an elder. Without this distinction, three things tend to go wrong:

First, *inequality* develops between staff and non-staff elders either in their minds or in how the congregation views them. Often, staff elders come to be regarded as the "real" pastors and the non-staff as mere advisors.

Second, the ghastly phenomenon of *professional pastoring* is propagated, whereby a man thinks of eldering/pastoring more as a profession than a calling. Certainly, a middle- to long-term calling is often expressed as a profession, but pastors should never think of themselves as professionals. This feeds entitlement amongst pastors and promotes institutionalism in the church.

And third, *staff management* is compromised. Imagine that an elder's staff role mostly involved elder/pastor responsibilities, such as care and counseling, oversight of Small Groups, and teaching theology classes. Imagine that he was a solid elder in terms of character and basic competencies, but that for some reason he no longer warranted his role on staff – maybe as the church grew it became clear he was too weak a delegator to warrant a staff position, or, maybe he was good at his job but the church hit financial problems and he needed to be laid off. If there was no distinction between his office of elder and his staff role, it would be hard to lay him off without it feeling like an indictment of him as an elder. Also, who would make the decision? It is not fair for the staff management (often the lead elder and/or executive elder) to be held to account for staff effectiveness without having the authority to adjust staff roles when necessary, but they need to be able to make such adjustments without feeling they are de-eldering someone if they adjust or eliminate his staff role.

Therefore, I recommend that the eldership team (not the staff management team) is responsible for a man becoming an elder and being de-eldered if necessary, and the staff management team (not the elders) is responsible for someone (elder or not) becoming a staffer and being removed from the staff if necessary. Therefore, depending on the circumstances, it is possible that a staff elder could lose his job but remain on the eldership team as a non-staff elder. Having said all this, in view of the sensitivities and overlap, the staff management team would work carefully and consultatively with the elders if they were needing to significantly adjust or terminate the staff position of a staff elder.

REFLECTION

1. Are the staff in your church in danger of falling into either of the two "ditches" of inferiority or entitlement? If so, why is that, and what could be done to improve the situation?

2. In your own words summarize what is meant by a "fire-break" between the office of an elder and his staff role. Do you agree that such a fire-break is important? Explain.

CHAPTER 16
WITH ELDERS' WIVES

There are few things more heartening in church life than seeing buoyant, engaged, church-proud, people-loving elders' wives, motivated by love for Jesus and his Church rather than because their husband is an elder.

Judging from the references to elders' wives and children in 1 Timothy 3 and Titus 1, we may expect that most elders will be married, although nowhere in the Bible are single men ruled out of eldership. Certainly, it has been my experience that single elders can play a vital role on an eldership team. It has also been my experience that elders' wives play a significant role in terms of the tone and effectiveness of an eldership team. Before we look at biblical characteristics for elders' wives and some practical suggestions for elders and their wives, we need to talk about being "together on mission."

TOGETHER ON A MISSION

Ashleigh and I speak of both *my* (PJ's) calling to eldership, and *our* calling to eldership. This "both/and" comes from two biblical convictions. First, we believe the Bible affords us *gender-appropriate roles in the home and the church*. As a mother in our home Ashleigh has a bond with our sons that I could never replicate, and as a mother in the church she ministers in a way I could not (Titus 2:3-5). Similarly, my role as a father in our home and father (elder) in our church is not one that Ashleigh tries to play. Second, we believe the Bible calls us to *actively support one another in our respective roles*. Ashleigh is called to *help* me (Gen. 2:18), and if I am truly *loving* her (Eph. 5:31-33) then of course I will support her. The "blend" of these two beliefs has enabled Ashleigh to be very involved in my world as an elder, without her feeling the need to actually be an elder.

BIBLICAL CHARACTERISTICS

There is no formal biblical position of "elder's wife," but she plays a key role in both qualifying and helping her husband. The first thing the Bible says about an elder's wife is that there should *only be one of them* (1 Tim. 3:2, Titus 1:6)! Faithfulness in marriage is something that both the elder and his wife are responsible for, therefore an elder's wife will be a one-man-woman in every sense, with her mind, body, and unity of calling with her husband. Second, the Bible speaks about the importance of an elder *managing his household well* (1 Tim. 3:4-5). His wife would surely assist with this, helping the family grow together in a happy and godly manner.

In addition to these two characteristics that are implied from her husband's role, there are four more characteristics mentioned in 1 Timothy 3:11 to consider: "dignified, not slanderers, but sober-minded, faithful in all things." I concluded in Chapter 14 that the women mentioned in this verse could be either wives of deacons or women deacons. If they are wives of deacons, then given their weightier responsibility, wives of elders should also have these characteristics. If they are women deacons, then given our aspirations for elders' wives to own and assist their husband's ministries as elders, then they would surely require these sorts of characteristics.

Dignified means being worthy of respect. If part of the basis for respecting an elder is his faithful marriage and well-managed home, then it follows that his wife will also be worthy of respect. Whether an extrovert or introvert, highly gifted or below average, having many children or none, having an easy or a tough life, the trend of her life will be worthy of respect. Attempts at perfection are not only bound to fail, but actually make it harder for people to respect you. True respect develops when you see someone struggle with similar things you do, but struggle in a God-glorifying manner. That kind of godly dignity is what makes other women feel "I can be like that" rather than "I could never be like that."

Slander is a catch-all bucket for any type of inappropriate speech about someone else. It might be saying something untrue, or partially true, or true but said with a wrong attitude or in an inappropriate context. Elders' wives can be uniquely tempted to slander as they will be aware of confidential things about people, and from time to time their husbands (and sometimes themselves) will be unfairly treated by people. Therefore, they need to be particularly disciplined in not slandering. They may draw strength from the example of Jesus, who did not retaliate to unfair accusations, entrusting himself instead to his heavenly Father.

Sober-mindedness means not being given to extremes in emotion or behavior. In view of the pressures of her life and her husband's calling, she will have ample provocation to be emotionally unstable! How might she regulate her emotions and behavior? By detaching from unpredictable things (e.g. the bank balance, her friends' moods, her children's behavior, and so on) and attaching to the only truly predictable thing in life – the Rock of Ages, Jesus Christ. Such sobriety of emotion and consistent behavior makes elders' wives pillars of strength in their families and church communities.

And, elders' wives should be *faithful in all things*. Note, it doesn't say perfect in all things, or better than the other women in the church at all things, but that she will be *faithful* in all things. She will be reliable in what she does. She will be a reliable wife and mother, a reliable church member, reliable in keeping confidences, and if she has a job beyond the home, she will be known for reliability there too. *Faithfulness* is especially important for an elder's wife because it is a fundamental Christian characteristic, and therefore something that both elders and their wives need to be particularly good at modeling (1 Cor. 4:2, Gal. 5:22, 1 Tim. 1:12, 2 Tim. 2:2). Also, eldership is a marathon not a sprint, requiring steady faithfulness in the same direction.

SUGGESTIONS TO ELDERS' WIVES

Remember there is no official position of "elder's wife," so when your husband becomes an elder you don't need to start dressing differently or take over the Children's Ministry! If you do take over the Children's Ministry, do it because you want to not because "it is something that an elder's wife should do." Don't feel pressured to do the "elder-wife thing." It isn't actually a thing. Be yourself.

Keep being the best possible member of your local church. I am sure you were trying to do this before your husband became an elder, because you love Jesus and his church. Keep doing this. Keep being "faithful in all things." There are few things better in church life than seeing buoyant, engaged, church-proud, people-loving elders' wives, motivated by love for Jesus and his Church rather than "because my husband is an elder."

Keep being the best wife you can be. If ever there was role that required a good helper, being an elder would be it (Gen. 2:18). Pray for your husband, encourage him, offer perspective on things in the church, work together with him in appropriate pastoral situations, and generally support him and his fellow elders as they lead the church forward.

SUGGESTIONS TO ELDERS

Be the best possible husband you can be. Love your wife as Christ loved the church. Delight in her. Support her in her calling in life. Be more imaginative and faithful in your leadership of the home than you are in your leadership of the church.

Be clear on your position concerning the role of women in the church. Confusion here will confuse and disempower your wife and other women in the church.

Involve your wives. They can offer you invaluable perspective, and the more ownership they feel around eldership, the more supportive they will be of their husbands. A practical way of involving wives is to schedule regular times together as "elders and wives." Some teams gather like this weekly or monthly, whilst others only gather several times a year. These times can be a mixture of fellowship and prayer for each other and the church, and discussion around suitable aspects of church life. The gatherings can be as simple as evenings together, or as elaborate as weekends away.

Don't pressure your wives to get together as a group by themselves unless they have an appetite for that, and unless one of them has the stature and gifting to lead those times well (this doesn't necessarily have to be the lead elder's wife). Also, they need to be explicitly committed to avoiding becoming a clique in the church, as women can be particularly sensitive to this.

REFLECTION

1. Generally speaking, do you feel your elders' wives are under-engaged, over-engaged, or correctly engaged? Explain.

2. What could be done to improve their level of engagement?

Elders

PART 5

ROLES

Elders

OVERVIEW OF PART 5

There are many different ways to divide up the roles of elders. Those fond of alliteration may enjoy *Guard-Guide-Govern* or *Character-Charisma-Competence-Chemistry*, or Phil Newton's *Doctrine-Discipline-Direction-Distinction*. Although lacking cadence, I think of elders as playing the following roles:

- **Shepherding** the flock (1 Pet. 5:2)

- **Teaching** the word (Titus 1:9)

- **Equipping** the saints (Eph. 4:11-12)

- **Leading**/governing zealously (Rom. 12:8, 1 Tim. 5:17, Heb. 13:17)

- Modeling Christian **character** and leadership (1 Tim. 3:2-7, Titus 1:5-8, 1 Pet. 5:1-4)

I feel that *all five must be explicitly articulated* to avoid any getting "lost" in the assumption that they are part of one of the others. For example, shepherding and teaching without leading tends to create a well-taught and well-cared for church that is missionally ineffective in the wider community. An apparently well led and well-equipped church with elders who are light on godly character is an accident waiting to happen. A team of elders who have impeccable character but who lack gifting to teach and equip will create an integrous yet impeded church.

We will look at the first four roles in the subsequent chapters, and dedicate all of Part 6 to modeling Christian character and leadership.

CHAPTER 17

SHEPHERD

The whole image of shepherding is characterized by intimacy, tenderness, skill, hard work, and love.
— Alexander Strauch

As a fellow elder to elders Peter wrote, "Shepherd the flock of God that is among you" (1 Pet. 5:2). Of the various words used to describe an elder's role, shepherd might be the richest. Although a less understood profession today than in biblical times, most are aware of the basic responsibilities a shepherd has: feeding, leading to pasture, protecting, herding, retrieving, shearing and grooming, and helping ewes give birth. The image is easy to understand, as one can readily imagine elders leading, feeding and loving God's people.

HUMBLE. HARD. HONORABLE.

Throughout history, shepherding has been a *humble* profession. Shepherds usually find themselves at the bottom end of society, usually poorly educated, and often impoverished immigrant workers. In developed economies today, many shepherds try to side-step the term "shepherd" altogether, preferring more sophisticated descriptions such as farmers, ranchers or livestock owners. Similarly, shepherding God's flock is humble work, and our recognition and reward will only be realized when the chief Shepherd appears, and we receive the unfading crown of glory (1 Pet. 5:4).

It is also a *hard* profession. Craig Roberts, a shepherd on the foothills of the Blue Ridge mountains in Virginia, USA, wrote, "Lambing ... often occurs at night, in the cold, and is a solitary farming task where the reward is personal satisfaction in perhaps saving a life of a ewe or bringing a lamb into the world that otherwise would not make it."[33] Eldership is not easy. The constant burden of responsibility for God's people, and the physical toll of time and energy spent on overseeing and caring for the congregation, is no small thing.

And yet it is a truly *honorable* endeavor. God, to whom all honor is due, refers to himself as our shepherd (Ps. 23, Jn. 10, 1 Pet. 5:4). The apostle Paul refers to shepherding as a *noble* task (1 Tim. 3:1). And when we consider the nobility of God's flock whom we serve – a chosen race, a royal priesthood, a people for his own possession – the nobility of our role is further magnified (1 Pet. 2:9).

LEARNING FROM THE LORD, MY SHEPHERD (PSALM 23)

Psalm 23, written by David, is about how the Lord shepherded David, and by implication how the Lord shepherds every believer. Because elders are under-shepherds of the Lord, and because we strive to shepherd God's flock in keeping with how the Lord shepherds his flock, there is much elders can learn from this psalm.

We learn that shepherds themselves have a heavenly shepherd – "the Lord is my shepherd" (v. 1). When I was eight years old, our family traveled from England to America on the renowned cruise liner, the QE2. I remember the experience well, including a vivid memory of being told the story of how once, on a cruise ship similar to the QE2, the passengers gathered one evening to entertain themselves with what we would call today an "open mic." A famous Shakespearian actor was aboard, and the passengers prevailed on him to recite something for them. Although not a religious man, he recited Psalm 23. His pitch, pace and pause were perfect. Following the applause, a doddery old woman took to the platform, and to everyone's surprise also started to recite Psalm 23. She stumbled over the words. Her pitch, pace and pause were appalling. After the smattering of slightly embarrassed applause, a person quietly asked the renowned actor what he made of it. He replied, "I know the psalm, but she knows the Shepherd." The Pharisees found themselves in a similar position, knowing God's word rather well and yet not knowing God himself. Let elder-shepherds know their Great Shepherd well, and let them shepherd others out of their own experience of being personally shepherded by God. The more we can personally say "The Lord is *my* shepherd" the more we will be able to help others say the same.

We learn that satisfaction can only be found in the chief shepherd – "I shall not want" (v. 1). David found satisfaction in the Lord. As elder-shepherds, our only hope of satisfying our flock is to shepherd them towards the Great Shepherd, Jesus, "the Shepherd and Overseer of [our] souls" (1 Pet. 2:25). His pasture alone satisfies. His water alone quenches thirst. His fold alone is secure. All our shepherding should be in a Christ-like direction, for only in Christ can anyone say, "I shall not want."

We learn that shepherds create a secure and restful environment – "He makes me lie down in green pastures. He leads me beside still waters…. You prepare a table for me in the presence of my enemies" (v. 2, 5). In its own way, David's world was as dangerous, anxious and hectic as ours, and yet he found solace in the Lord. Elder-shepherds should ensure their churches are places of tranquility and rest for their flock replete with "tables" laden with spiritual sustenance. God's word is our food. God's Spirit is our drink. God's flock are our comrades-in-arms. Our gatherings refresh and equip us to go back out behind enemy lines.

We learn that shepherding is fundamentally about restoration – "he restores my soul … you anoint my head with oil" (v. 3, 5). Because God is about restoring people, elder-shepherds are about the same. Elders ooze restoration in their actions, attitudes, words and prayers. We encourage more than criticize. We instruct rather than condemn. We bless rather than curse. We believe the best. We forgive seventy times seven times. We pursue the wandering sheep. We instruct the wayward with all tenderness. And, we *anoint heads with oil.* Middle Eastern shepherds would rub their sheep's heads with olive oil to kill off harmful insects prone to lodge there. Similarly, we rub the oil of the gospel into our people's heads to fumigate against spiritual disease.

We learn that shepherding involves guarding – "even though I walk through the valley of the shadow of death, I will fear no evil, for you are with me; your rod and staff they comfort me" (v. 4). David knew that although his enemy was watching for him, God was watching for his enemy. He knew God had a rod to defend him from his foes, and a staff to lift him up after a fall (a staff was a long stick with a hook on the end of it). Similarly, elder-shepherds are called to guard the flock and to guard themselves. This is an important aspect of eldering which we will look at in greater detail in a moment.

LEARNING FROM THE GOOD SHEPHERD (JOHN 10)

More than half of John chapter 10 consists of Jesus speaking about his role as our Good Shepherd. As with Psalm 23, elders have much to learn from this passage about how to be under-shepherds in Christ's flock.

We learn of the importance of the shepherd's voice – "the sheep follow him for they know his voice" (v. 4). God's word is the means by which we are born into the flock of God (Jn. 10:27-28, Jas. 1:18), and also the means by which we *follow* our shepherd from that moment forward. Under-shepherds have the great privilege of teaching God's word to God's flock. When their voice is rich in God's word, it will be compelling and attractive, and their sheep will not be tempted to eat at the hand of a false teacher – "a stranger they will not follow, but they will flee from him, for they do not know the voice of strangers" (v. 5).

We learn of the importance of personal connection between the shepherd and the sheep – "he calls his own sheep by name and leads them out" (v. 3). Being personally known by the Good Shepherd is a privileged reality for a child of God, and is a reality that under-shepherds would strive to replicate in how they care for their sheep. Craig Roberts explains that good shepherds pay attention to both the flock and the individual:

> Providing clean water, ample forage and shelter to an entire flock is essential to maintaining the health of the flock. But the success of a shepherd … is in the compassion they have for each individual. This means being able to identify a sick or injured sheep or lamb within a flock of hundreds or thousands of sheep … The more concern the shepherd has for the individuals who are in need of health care, supplemental food assistance or individual attention, the healthier the flock and the more profitable the whole operation is.[34]

In a smaller church, it is possible that without much organization each member will feel meaningfully connected to at least one elder-shepherd. But in a larger church it is usually best to organize the flock into smaller pastoral units to ensure that each sheep feels a sufficient connection to at least one elder-shepherd, and a very meaningful connection to someone helping the elder to shepherd that section of the church, such as a Small Group leader. Sheep can easily wander after any number of unhelpful things, such as money and false knowledge (1 Tim. 6:10, 20-21), and need a shepherd to keep a loving eye on them, and help retrieve them when they wander (Lk. 15:1-7, Jas. 5:19-20).

Whilst there is no substitute for individual shepherding, it is also important that the elders – especially the lead elder – are skilled at shepherding the entire flock. When the entire flock is moving in a deliberate direction at a purposeful pace, individual sheep tend to be less distracted and less prone to wander. A collective sense of vision, purpose and momentum creates an environment where less individual shepherding is required.

We learn how a shepherd guards the flock – "the good shepherd lays down his life for the sheep" (v. 11). When a shepherd brought his flock back to the fold after a day of grazing, he would sleep lying across the open door to ensure that predators could not enter without first alerting him, and giving him the opportunity to fight them off. Quite literally, he laid his life down for the sheep. With this picture in mind, Jesus describes a trio of adversaries. The first is the thief who tries to sneak into the fold through an opening other than the door, to steal, kill and destroy (v. 1, 10). The second is the wolf who tries to snatch and scatter the sheep (v. 12). The third is the hired hand who, unlike a true shepherd, flees for his own life when he sees a wolf coming, because "he cares nothing for the sheep" (v. 13). Although the context concerns Christ's role in defending his worldwide flock on a macro scale, this is significantly outworked on a micro scale by the Lord's under-shepherds guarding the sheep in their local church.

GUARDING

The theme of guarding came up in both Psalm 23 and John 10, and Jesus said in Matthew 7:15, "Beware of false prophets, who come to you in sheep's clothing but inwardly are ravenous wolves." The apostle Paul charged the Ephesian elders in a similar manner: "I know that after my departure, fierce wolves will come in among you, not sparing the flock; and from among your own selves will arise men speaking twisted things, to draw away the disciples after them. Therefore, be alert…" (Acts 20:29-31). We will now look at how elder-shepherds should guard against heresy, guard against thieves and wolves, and also guard themselves.

Guarding against heresy

Paul commanded Timothy and Titus to "keep a close watch on yourself and on the teaching" and to "hold firm to the trustworthy word as taught, so that he may be able to give instruction in sound doctrine and also to rebuke those who contradict it" (1 Tim. 4:16, Titus 1:9). The word of God is sacred, and its true meaning should be safeguarded. Both truth and lies are powerful. Wonky doctrine produces wonky lives. Dangerous doctrine produces dangerous lives. Sound doctrine produces sound lives. Elders are to guard against outright heresy as well as unhelpful imbalances that can, over time, distort the truth and harm the flock. Whilst not every elder needs to be a theological giant, he cannot be a theological midget, and must be able to rightly handle the word of truth (2 Tim. 2:15). And, every eldership team ideally needs at least one theological giant on the team, or helping the team.

Guarding against thieves and wolves

Thieves and wolves may well take the form of false teachers (Matt. 7:15, Acts 20:29-31), or they might be sexually immoral or divisive people who need to either be brought to repentance or removed (1 Cor. 5:1-13, Rom. 16:17, Titus 3:10-11). They might be men who come into the church with the intention of preying on weak women (2 Tim. 3:5-9). They might be those who, like Diotrephes, sought position out of ungodly ambition (3 Jn. 1:9). Or, they might be anyone who continues in willful, unrepentant behavior that will damage their own soul and the flock (Matt. 18:15-18).

Elder-shepherds should stand guard at the various "doors" into the church. They need to be thoughtful around what books and resources they recommend, and be alert to who their people are listening to online. They need to keep watch on all the different ministries in the church to ensure that they are faithfully representing the doctrine, vision and values of the church. And most importantly, they need to be properly engaged and alert in the process of welcoming new members into the church.

Elder-shepherds need great wisdom and courage to guard the church. In some situations, prayerful watchfulness is all that is required. In other situations, "correcting [your] opponents with gentleness" will suffice (2 Tim. 2:25, Gal. 6:1). Sometimes, offenders are best discipled and restored through remaining in membership but refraining from any form of leadership for a season. Other times, public rebuke is necessary (1 Tim. 5:20). And sometimes, people "must be silenced" and even removed from fellowship (Titus 1:11, 1 Cor. 5:12-13). Space does not permit a fuller treatment of church discipline here, but I would urge eldership teams to avoid the two extremes of *gun shy* or *trigger happy*. Church discipline is an essential component of eldering, and eldership teams must give patient and unhurried thought to what principles they will seek to follow when different situations arise. However, each situation will be different, and even with a decent grip on the biblical principles of church discipline, elders will need great wisdom to find a proportional response, factoring in things like the nature of the offence, the position of the person in the church, and the degree of repentance.

Guarding themselves

Paul spoke more than once about the importance of elders guarding themselves. He told the Ephesian elders, "Pay careful attention to yourselves and to all the flock," and told Timothy, "Keep a close watch on yourself and on the teaching" (Acts 20:28, 1 Tim. 4:16). The logic is strong: if the shepherd is taken out, either due to his own action or that of others, then the sheep will get scratched at best and scattered at worst. Therefore, elders understand that a key part of guarding the flock is guarding themselves, and holding each other to account. I find it helpful to think of four concentric "circles" of accountability for myself and my fellow elders:

Circle 1: The Man: This is the most important circle, because accountability hinges on my personal honesty, and not a system. If I am not honest and open, then no system, or set of questions, or caring friends will make me so.

Circle 2: The Team: Our eldership team is our primary circle of accountability. We think of accountability mainly as encouraging each other and enhancing each other's strengths, but also about confrontation and correction when necessary. We find that the following things help create an atmosphere on our team where accountability thrives:

- We *celebrate the gospel*. A non-legalistic, grace-enthused, gospel-centered approach to life promotes loving Jesus and hating sin. Legalism is fertilizer for sin, whilst grace provides a hot-house for holiness (Titus 2:11-14).

- Our relationships are *intentional but not intense*. Vulnerability and honesty are a way of life. We try to laugh a lot, and care for each other. A brotherly atmosphere fosters heart-level accountability, as opposed to an officious atmosphere that hinders it. We often build in time in elders' meetings to ask each other how we are doing, and to pray for each other. If our agenda is too busy for that, then we either work smarter, or lengthen the meeting, or meet more regularly, but one way or another, we are determined to keep brotherhood a central part of our team dynamic.

- We have meaningful connection as *married couples*. Wives often sense anxiety in each other's lives quicker than men do, and tend to be quicker in calling for help than their husbands.

- We are all clear that any of us can raise issues with another elder(s) anytime *without fear or prejudice*.

The plurality of an eldership team goes a long way to self-correcting internal blind spots and weaknesses and generally keeping the team self-accountable. However, it does not go the whole way, and a wise and humble eldership team will also recognize the following two circles of accountability.

Circle 3: Our Congregation: Although our eldership team is clear that we are authorized to lead our congregation, we remain alert to the perspective and concerns of our congregation. We make sure our people know that they may raise concerns about an elder, with any other elder, at any time, without fear of rebuff. We encourage our members to follow the Matthew 18 principle of first taking their concern to the individual elders with whom they have issue, but we also recognize that this is sometimes virtually impossible for a congregant to do[35] which is why we say they are welcome to talk to any elder about any elder any time. Some churches opt for a formal 'grievance policy,' whilst others operate less formally, but either way, clear thought and communication needs to happen before the fact, or you will have the added strain of trying to work out helpful protocol amidst the pressure cooker of accusation or strife.

Circle 4: Outside Advisors: The Roman poet, Juvenal, asked the question, *Quis custodiet ipsos custodes* – "Who guards the guards?"[36] A significant part of our answer to that question is having several trusted church leaders from our network who regularly help us with philosophy and practice of ministry, and help enhance a healthy atmosphere on our eldership team. We give these brothers a standing invitation to bring any ideas or concerns to us at any time. All the elders know these brothers, not just me, and an ever-increasing number of our members know them also. These brothers often see things, and say things, that are trickier for us to either see or say. And, they can ask questions that make us think ahead of time about things that we otherwise might blunder into blindly – prevention is better than cure. A standing invitation doesn't mean that they will show up unannounced, or that they will in any way usurp the God-given authority of our local team of elders, but it does mean that they are empowered to watch our backs. I have told my fellow elders that they are warmly encouraged to talk to any of our outside advisors any time about anything, even without talking to me first if they would find that easier.

Over two decades of working with multiple eldership teams, I have consistently found that the four circles work together to create a natural, un-intense, effective safety net of accountability. Because accountability is an issue of the heart, there is actually no fool-proof human way of ensuring leaders and elders remain accountable, but overdoing it, or doing it in the wrong way, makes things worse because it promotes control, fear, and legalism which are fertile soil for all sorts of sins and dysfunctionalities to thrive.

You might have noticed that within the four circles I didn't explicitly mention things like regular performance reviews, or well-worded Constitutions that limit certain people's power. Such things may well be useful, but they are not as effective as the four circles (assuming each of the circles are mostly working right). And if one isn't working (or doesn't exist), it is better to bolster the circle in question than to boost legislation.

Guarding through prayer

Prayer should be our *priority*. We read in Acts 6:4, "But we will devote ourselves to prayer and to the ministry of the word." At this early stage in the Jerusalem church, the apostles were leading as the *de facto* elders. The church had grown, and growth had brought the need for more organization and more leaders. A key motivation for appointing additional leaders was so that the "elders" could safeguard their devotion to two things: prayer and ministry of the word. If we were to survey the amount of time, energy and conviction that eldership teams around the world today direct to the ministry of the word, I think we would be fairly encouraged. But I am less sure if we would celebrate the results of a similar survey on prayer. This should not be. Prayer must be our priority.

Prayer is also our *privilege*. When I think back on years and years of elders' meetings, the memories that rise most rapidly in my mind are our times of prayer. The heat of prayer welded us into a unified brotherhood. The nature of prayer kept us free from burdens that were not ours but the Lord's to carry. The discipline of prayer kept us focused on what was truly important. The presence of God kept us soft-hearted but thick-skinned. As we prayed, things became clear and despair yielded to hope. As we prayed, we cast our burdens, refreshed our souls, and stoked our fires of faith. And as we prayed, God moved for "by prayer the church on earth has at its disposal the powers of the heavenly world."[37]

And crucially, prayer *protects* us from our propensity to self-reliance. Time spent in prayer is conclusive evidence that we really believe that we can bear no lasting fruit outside of Christ

(Matt. 16:18, Jn. 15:4). Prayer is the stake in the heart of our self-sufficiency, and a declaration to the heavenlies that we really believe that unless the Lord builds the house we labor in vain (Ps. 127:1). "We'll pray at the end if there is time" are words that should be outlawed from elders' meetings. Rather pray upfront. Rather let other items fall off the agenda. Brothers, it is essential that we are committed to the priority, privilege and protection of prayer. Prayer must underpin and soak all that we do. Without prayer our shepherding, teaching, equipping and leading will be in our own strength rather than in the Lord's.

TWO TENSIONS TO MAINTAIN

As we close out this chapter on shepherding, here are two important tensions to maintain:

First, neither under-estimate or over-estimate the wisdom and strength of the sheep. Sheep are not as dumb as folklore suggests. They are walking within minutes of being born, they have an impressive memory, and their flocking mentality is more a genius survival mechanism than a sign of helplessness.[38] God's sheep are our brothers and sisters and gifted partners in ministry, and should be treated with respect not contempt. Equally, they need shepherds. They have no claws, teeth or turn of pace to defend themselves. They can have a limited sense of direction and can be prone to wander, and they can struggle to find pasture and water by themselves. Although they naturally flock together, they tend not to organize themselves well. Simply, we have the privileged and necessary role of guarding, guiding and governing them.

If this tension is not respected, elders can drift either into neglect or into hyper-shepherding. In terms of the latter, the "shepherding movement" of the 1970s and 1980s arose out of a well-intentioned desire to shepherd people well by providing "covenant relationships" where accountability and stronger character development could flourish.

> Although the principle on which this movement was founded had biblical support, their practice exceeded biblical norms. In time, the movement gained a reputation for an overemphasis on the importance of obedience to one's shepherd and in some cases, disobeying one's shepherd was tantamount to disobeying God. Throughout its churches, sheep often lacked the freedom to obey Scripture and their consciences because their "shepherd's" word was authoritative.[39]

Second, be both "hands-on" and "high-level." A shepherd must be simultaneously *amongst and over* his sheep (1 Thess. 5:12). If he is not sufficiently amongst his sheep, he will not spot the individual sheep who is sickening. If he is not sufficiently over his sheep, he will not spot the threat to the whole. Elders should preside diligently at a *high level* over policies, programs and budgets, as these things provide security and blessing for the whole flock. They also need to pastor the sheep in a *hands-on* way. Sheep are like walking strips of Velcro, and regularly need a shepherd's hands to help pick off the muck.

As I have already mentioned, I feel it is unhelpful to designate the staff elders "pastors" and the non-staff elders "elders," as this plays into the unhelpful arrangement where the staff do the *hands on* shepherding, whilst the busy, street-wise businessmen-elders do the *high-level* oversight. This will invariably lead to tensions between the two groups, and to imbalance, because effective high-level governance *requires* hands-on connection with the sheep, as much as hands-on connection with the sheep is enhanced by high-level governance. The New Testament knows nothing of such division of labor. Certainly, some elders might be skilled in one area more than the other, and some might give more time to one area than the other, but it is important that all elders are practitioners in some way in both areas.

REFLECTION

1. As you reflect on the humble, hard, yet honorable nature of shepherding, what emotions do you feel, and why?

2. What was your key takeaway from Psalm 23?

3. What was your key takeaway from John 10?

4. What are some of the practical ways that your eldership team guards against heresy?

5. What kinds of "thieves and wolves" does your eldership team need to be particularly on guard against in your context?

6. In terms of guarding yourselves, give answers to these two case studies:

- I am concerned that a fellow elder is close to burn out/drinking too much/flirting with another woman/ neglecting his marriage and kids. What steps should I take?

- A couple of us elders are concerned that our lead elder is not in a good place/becoming legalistic and heavy-handed. We have tried to gently and tactfully raise these concerns with him, but he doesn't appear to be listening. What steps should we take?

7. How is your team doing in terms of prayer? What mindsets or practical things need to change to ensure more prayer and better prayer?

8. Are you naturally more drawn to the high-level or hands on aspect of eldership? Briefly elaborate.

CHAPTER 18

TEACH

It is God's Word that gives life. A good pastor believes this, trusts this, and centers his ministry on this fact.
– Thabiti Anyabwile

Elders are clearly called to faithfully teach God's word and to refute heresy (1 Tim. 3:2, 2 Tim. 4:2, Acts 20:29-31, Titus 1:9). Phil Newton concurs that teaching is a defining mark of eldership: "The qualification distinguishing elders from deacons is the elder's aptness to teach and ability to engage others doctrinally, even those in disagreement."[40] Whether teaching from the Sunday pulpit, or in a class, small group, or one on one, elders need to be *convinced*, *competent* and *passionate* teachers.

CONVINCED

Elders need to be convinced of the centrality of teaching God's word to their ministry, and "hold firm to the trustworthy word as taught" (Titus 1:9). They need to be convinced that they continue the great tradition of Christian leaders who have always taught God's word. Teaching God's truth is as old as humanity itself. Abel and Abraham were referred to as prophets (Lk. 11:50-51, Gen. 20:7), and Moses and Joshua proclaimed and applied the covenant truths of God to Israel (Deut. 5 onwards, Josh. 24). With the development of the temple, the priests became the primary teachers of God's word, punctuated through the centuries by the itinerant preaching ministry of Old Testament prophets. Then, the New Testament commences with the powerful preaching ministry of John the Baptist, who paved the way for the greatest preacher of them all, Jesus Christ.

Someone once said that God only had one Son and he made him a preacher. Jesus announced his ministry as primarily one of proclaiming God's word (Lk. 4:18), and then proceeded to do just that for three years. He taught his disciples privately and the crowds publicly. When he encountered multitudes "like sheep without a shepherd," his solution was to *teach* them (Mk. 6:34). When the crowds swelled due to his miracles, he would diligently re-focus on preaching – "Let us go on to the next towns, that I may preach there also, for that is why I came out" (Mk. 1:38). At the end of his earthly ministry, he commissioned Peter to *feed* his lambs and *feed* his sheep, and commissioned his disciples to go and make disciples of all nations, *teaching* them to obey all he had commanded them (Matt. 28:20).

The apostles and elders of the New Testament obeyed Christ's command and committed themselves to preaching and teaching. The ministry of the word was so central to church life that Luke often referred to the advance of the gospel as the advance of the *word of God* (Acts 6:7). The leaders of the Jerusalem church delegated various ministries so that they could devote themselves to "prayer and the ministry of the word" (Acts 6:4), and Paul announced a curse on himself if he forfeited his preaching ministry – "Woe is me if I do not preach the gospel" (1 Cor. 9:16). His logic was compelling – "how are they to hear without someone preaching?" (Rom. 10:14), and his final charge to Timothy should convince all elders in every generation about the importance of teaching God's word:

> I charge you in the presence of God and of Christ Jesus, who is to judge the living and the dead, and by his appearing and his kingdom: preach the word; be ready in season and out of season; reprove, rebuke, and exhort, with complete patience and teaching. For the time is coming when people will not endure sound teaching, but having itching ears they will

accumulate for themselves teachers to suit their own passions, and will turn away from listening to the truth and wander off into myths. As for you, always be sober-minded, endure suffering, do the work of an evangelist, fulfill your ministry (2 Tim. 4:1-5).

COMPETENT

"Rightly handling the word of truth" (2 Tim. 2:15) requires competence. Sometimes elders need to wield the word like a scalpel, and other times like a hammer. They need to be able to straddle what John Stott calls the paradoxes of preaching, such as being both authoritative and tentative, prophetic and pastoral, thoughtful and passionate, and bringing both timeless truth and contemporary application.

Whilst all elders will surely teach in some contexts, 1 Timothy 5:17 suggests that some elders will teach more than others in the major gatherings. But whatever the context, the most important thing is to *say what the text says* rather than saying what you want it to say. Charles Simeon explains, "My endeavor is to bring out of Scripture what is there and not to thrust in what I think might be there. I have a great jealousy on this head; never to speak more or less than I believe to be the mind of the Spirit in the passage I am expounding."[41] Similarly, former Archbishop of Canterbury Donald Coggan said, "The Christian preacher has a boundary set for him. When he enters the pulpit, he is not an entirely free man.... [T]he Almighty has set him his bounds that he shall not pass."[42]

Some might say that each preacher needs to determine himself what he thinks the meaning of each passage is, especially through asking the Holy Spirit for revelation. Certainly, the Holy Spirit plays a key role in our preparation and delivery, and our culture and context will have a considerable bearing on what we consider to be the key emphasis in any text. However, a teacher's main task is to try and faithfully preach what God's word is saying rather than what he wants to say! To this end, the following questions are helpful to ask when approaching a text:

- *What is the historical context?* Who was the writer? Who was the audience? What was their unique context? Why was it written to *them*?

- *What is the literary context?* What light do the verses before and after the text shed on the text? What light do the main themes of the book in which the text is situated shed on the text?

- *What is the structure of the passage?* Does the structure of the passage shed light on the meaning of the text? Are there any key words, figures of speech, imagery, or repetition, that help our understanding of the passage?

- *Is there a primary thought or intention of the passage?* If there is a primary emphasis, then make that the primary emphasis of your message. If there are several key thoughts but no stand-out thought, then structure your message accordingly.

- *How has the church understood and applied this passage over the years?* What can we learn from the commentators, the church fathers, and from the witness of God's people over the ages? Is what I am saying novel? If so, it may well be wrong!

Once you have asked and answered these questions, you are well positioned to ask two more:

- *How can I apply the meaning of the text to the audience?* Sloppiness with application is a serious thing. Jesus called hearers-not-doers "foolish" and James called them "deceived" (Matt. 7:27, Jas. 1:22). Some points of application may be obvious from the passage, and others can be drawn from your knowledge of your people and their context, but one way or another we are to help "connect biblical truth to hopes, narratives, fears, and errors of people in that particular time and place."[43] Pray for the Holy Spirit's help in this. Some weeks you may help apply specific things to different groups, and other weeks you might give broader application. Some weeks you might be direct, rugged, and penetrating, and other weeks less explicit, trusting the Holy Spirit to bring appropriate application to each person. Some weeks you might explain and apply as you go, other weeks you might store up the application for the end.

- *How does the text connect to the meta-narrative of the Bible, the gospel?*[44] In what way does the text reflect or anticipate the gospel of Jesus? Is there typology or analogy that points to Jesus? How can you present the message to believers and unbelievers in a non-moralistic, gospel-centered manner?

PASSIONATE

Theological precision should be augmented with passion and faith. Doubting and disillusioned teachers will not reap. Teachers who make orthodoxy their goal rather than saved souls and changed hearts, will not reap. Martyn Lloyd-Jones referred to some preachers as "perfectly orthodox, perfectly useless."[45] Orthodoxy should not be knocked, but maybe those who hide behind it as an excuse for dry, ineffectual preaching should be! Mere Bible-explaining is not enough. Consider the phrase *expositional preaching*: those more enamored with the first word should work hard on the second, as much as those more enamored with the second should work hard on the first.

By passionate I do not necessarily mean loud or angry. Our goal is to be *effective* not *offensive*. But the word of God *is* "living and active, sharper than any two-edged sword, piercing to the division of soul and of spirit, of joints and of marrow, and discerning the thoughts and intentions of the heart" (Heb. 4:12), and will therefore sometimes be offensive. Insipid moralism and cute platitudes will not penetrate the bastion of men's hearts or dissipate the fog of modern-day liberalism, but the word of God will. It is razor sharp. Supernaturally sharp. It will wake the dead and re-shape souls. Therefore, we are passionate in our proclamation of these God-breathed "sacred writings, which are able to make you wise for salvation through faith in Christ Jesus" (2 Tim. 3:15). We passionately believe that "Good preaching shapes lives. It renews and reforms churches to become forces to be reckoned with. It can even transform whole towns, communities, or even nations, as the marvelous legacy of church history can demonstrate."[46] As Spurgeon urges, "We have only to have faith in God's Word, and speak it out straight, and we shall see proud rebels yielding. No mind is so desperately set on mischief, so resolutely opposed to Christ that it cannot be made to bow before the power of the words of God."[47]

REFLECTION

1. Write a few sentences around your convictions about the centrality of teaching to eldership.

2. How would you describe your current level of competence as a teacher of God's word? Are you naturally stronger at exposition or application? What could you do to improve the one you are weaker at? Do you have a framework you use to approach a text? Elaborate.

3. What excites you and challenges you about preaching simultaneously to believers and unbelievers in a non-moralist, gospel-centered manner?

4. What things do you find increase and decrease your passion for teaching God's word?

CHAPTER 19
EQUIP

The ministry of equipping revolutionizes all aspects of eldering, busting the eldership bottleneck and making elders multipliers of ministry.

OVERSEERS NOT OVERDOERS

Although ultimate responsibility lies with the elders for spiritual and general matters in the church, this does not mean elders should monopolize ministry and leadership in the church. The term "overseer" is helpful here – overseer not overdoer! Elders must equip and empower others to lead. To equip means to enable, to fit out, to train in such a way that one can operate without constant oversight or assistance. In Ephesians 4:11-16, "the Magna Carta of church ministry … the blueprint of God's living temple,"[48] the apostle Paul identifies "equipping the saints" as the essence of Christian leadership. Not only does he use the word "equip" twice (v. 12 and v. 16), but the passage crescendos with the intention that the body builds *itself* up in love, something that is only possible if the parts of the body are equipped.

Pastor-teachers (elders) need to be clear on this: *a vital goal of church leadership is to equip the saints for ministry*. Sometimes eldering will involve duties that do not directly equip anyone, and certainly, some aspects of eldering should not be relinquished to others. Nonetheless, our ultimate agenda is equipping others to do the work of the ministry. This a challenge for several reasons. First, it requires effort, as it always takes more energy and innovation to equip and delegate than to *do* the work oneself. Second, to the small-minded and insecure, it can appear to be a threat to job security. (It actually never is, as multiplied ministry requires more oversight, not less). And third, society – certainly in the West – is generally resistant. John MacArthur diagnoses America today as "the most narcissistic, self-absorbed, self-centered society that America has ever known and becoming increasingly more so, if that is possible."[49] This tempts elders to capitulate to the curse of clericalism, creating churches where they are the only ones equipped to do the work of the ministry, whilst normal believers sit back and applaud or criticize their ministry, seldom participating other than maybe to pay their dues. How tragically like 1 Samuel 14:22, where on the day of battle the only ones equipped with swords were King Saul and Prince Jonathan!

Here in Ephesians 4, and in his wider writings, Paul leaves us in no doubt about his anti-clericalist views. The purpose of church leadership is not to *protect its own* but to *promote the people*. Every believer is "in the ministry," every believer is a minister, and therefore every believer needs to be equipped and released into ministry. And there is a great deal of equipping that needs to be done, for it is the saints, not pastors specifically, who are charged to exhort one another every day to protect against the deceitfulness of sin and help maintain our confidence in salvation to the end (Heb. 3:12-14). It is regular saints, not pastors, who are charged to "stir up one another to love and good works, not neglecting to meet together, as is the habit of some, but encouraging one another, and all the more as you see the Day drawing near (Heb. 10:24-25). It is regular saints, not pastors, who are charged to bear one another's burdens, confess to each other, and pray for each other (Gal. 6:2, Jas. 5:16). It is regular saints, not pastors *per se*, who are called to teach and admonish one another in all wisdom (Col. 3:16).

And what of their ministry to those outside the church? Regular believers are called to walk wisely and properly before outsiders to make the most of every opportunity (Col. 4:5, 1 Thess. 4:12). John Calvin clarifies that *all* believers "should seek to bring others into the church, and should strive to lead the wanderers back to the road, should stretch forth a hand to the fallen and should win over the outsiders."[50] There is an immense need for elders to equip the saints to do the work of the ministry, and resurrect the glorious doctrine of the priesthood of all believers held so dear by the Reformers:

> [F]or Luther, the priesthood of all believers did not mean, "I am my own priest." It meant rather: In the community of saints, God has so tempered the body that we are all priests to each other. We stand before God and intercede for one another, we proclaim God's Word to one another and celebrate His presence among us in worship, praise, and fellowship. Moreover, our priestly ministry does not terminate upon ourselves. It propels us into the world in service and witness.[51]

Carlyle Marney wrote in his book *Priests to Each Other*, "It was a great perversion of the Gospel that inserted a bastard individualism here and then taught us that the believers' priesthood meant that 'every tub must sit on its own bottom.'[52] Quoting this, Timothy George comments, "The priesthood of all believers is a call to ministry and service; it is a barometer of the quality of the life of God's people in the body of Christ and of the coherence of our witness in the world, the world for which Christ died."[53]

Elders are fathers of the family of God who combat this "bastard individualism" through equipping the saints for ministry.

PASTOR IS DIFFERENT FROM PASTORAL

As pastors, elders should not monopolize pastoral ministry. Nouns should result in verbs. Pastors should lead to people being *pastoral*. That doesn't mean everyone has to suddenly be called pastors, but it should mean that many are being steadily equipped and released into pastoral ministry. Some of the most pastorally effective churches I know have the majority of their pastoral work done by a *pastoral team* consisting of elders and non-elders (women and men). Such elders are not abdicating their responsibility to pastor the flock, they are fulfilling it. The church is a family, and healthy families require care from both fathers and mothers, and from brothers and sisters. Fathers should not dominate pastoral care themselves, but rather make sure it happens in a healthy and holistic family manner. This means actively releasing mothers and sisters and brothers into pastoral leadership and ministry. This is what *pastors* should do.

EQUIPPING IS DIFFERENT FROM TEACHING

I once received this email from an elder at a church that was world renowned for its strong pulpit ministry:

> We have heard/learned much as a church, but applied much less than we should have. In leading small groups for decades, I always feared the verse, "But be doers of the word, and not hearers only, deceiving yourselves" (James 1:22) … I see a slew of gifted men and women in this church waiting to be deployed.

This elder was acknowledging that it is possible for an apparently strong teaching ministry to be weak in actually equipping the saints. According to 2 Timothy 3:16-17, God's word rightly handled *should* result in the saints being equipped for every good work. If it doesn't, then maybe the teaching isn't as strong we thought! Jesus and James were scathing about hearing without doing (Matt. 7:24-27, Jas. 1:22-25), therefore those that speak should make it as easy as possible for the hearers to *do*. Teaching is not an end in itself, rather a means to the end of fulfilling the Great Commission, which is to teach people to *do* all that Jesus' commanded (Matt. 28:20). If the Great Commission was to *teach* them to *know*, then teaching without equipping would be fine. But it isn't, so it's not.

APPLICATION

I encourage elders to consider the following to fulfill their responsibility to *equip*.

First, *personally be active practitioners* of Christian life and leadership. It is hard to equip people in areas you have no experience in.

Second, *maintain a big vision*. If your vision is so big that you cannot fulfill it by yourself, you will be forced into equipping and releasing others.

Third, avoid *over-stating the role of pastors*, as this will gradually make the congregation passive, and place a weight of expectation on pastors that they were never designed to fulfill.

Fourth, keep your *shepherding model (pastoral care) simple, scalable and empowering of others*. If it isn't, the quality and quantity of pastoral care will be constricted by the capability and size of the eldership team. Also, try and keep the model flexible enough to allow different saints to express themselves differently, whilst still working cohesively together.

Fifth, keep the teaching ministry in the church strong in both *exegesis and application*.

Sixth, have a *clear leadership development strategy*. If you don't have a leadership development target to shoot at, you will certainly miss. Don't only have an elder development track, but have tracks to develop and release other men and women into different positions of leadership.

Finally, and very importantly, periodically brainstorm together how you can freshly *infuse each of the other roles of eldership with "equip."* For example, ask yourselves:

- As *shepherds*, how can we equip others to help us shepherd the flock?

- As *teachers*, how can we equip others to teach?

- As *leaders*, how can we equip others to lead in different areas of church life? Are we thinking radically enough? Are we thinking "triple it?" Are we reserving leadership in any area for either elders or men where the Bible does not explicitly reserve it?

REFLECTION

1. "Equip" is an often overlooked aspect of eldership, yet has the potential to revolutionize it. Do you agree or disagree? Explain.

2. Comment on the connection and distinction between teaching and equipping.

3. Which implications most caught your eye. Explain.

4. Where might your eldership team be a bottleneck? How could that be remedied?

CHAPTER 20

LEAD

If the local church was merely a flock in need of care, or a class in need of instruction, then conventional pastor-teacher activities would suffice. But if the local church is in fact God's army to push back darkness in neighborhoods and nations, then catalytic leadership is cardinal.

THE SPIRITUAL GIFT OF LEADERSHIP

The spiritual gift of leadership is available to any Christ-follower in any leadership position, whether in the home, at work, or in the church. As I have been saying, the gift of leadership is not only for elders in a church. In fact, a vital part of the elders' mandate is to empower many to lead in different areas of church. Eldership and leadership should not be synonymous, or else leadership of anyone who isn't an elder will be impeded. However, given their particular role, elders should be amongst those who most eagerly desire the spiritual gift of leadership. The clearest reference to the gift of leadership is Romans 12:6-8:

> Having gifts that differ according to the grace given to us, let us use them: if prophecy, in proportion to our faith; if service, in our serving; the one who teaches, in his teaching; the one who exhorts, in his exhortation; the one who contributes, in generosity; *the one who leads, with zeal*; the one who does acts of mercy, with cheerfulness.

I would define the gift of leadership as *the God-given ability to help move people and situations forward.* Here are several observations about the gift of leadership as it pertains to eldership:

It is a gift not a position. God gifts some people with a supernatural ability to lead. This is therefore an essential gift for an elder. Some elders, particularly the lead elder, will have a more pronounced leadership gift than others, but all elders need at least a touch of this gift. John Stott underlines this saying, "The New Testament never contemplates the grotesque situation in which the church commissions and authorizes people to exercise a ministry for which they lack both the divine call and the divine equipment."[54] The spiritual gift of leadership is essential equipment for elders. Elders can grow in their leadership gifting once they are appointed, but it is a mistake to appoint someone to eldership without first seeing some evidence of leadership gifting.

It is a gift not an issue of character. The Old Testament accounts of Samson and Saul leave us in no doubt of the difference between gifting and character. If the principle holds, it means that someone with a powerful leadership gift might not have sufficient character, and therefore will not make a good elder. It also means that someone with impeccable character might not have an ounce of leadership about him, and therefore might not make a good elder either. Trouble awaits any elder whose gifting writes checks his character can't cash.

It is a gift not a style. Like any spiritual gift, it will be expressed differently depending on personality and the context, but it is fundamentally a gift not a style. For example, some elders might express their leadership gift quite *boisterously*, and others more *subtly*. Some will express it *consciously*, whilst others will express it in a more *intuitive* way.[55]

It is different from the spiritual gift of teaching, which we will talk about below.

DIFFERENT FROM THE SPIRITUAL GIFT OF TEACHING

It is quite common for elders, particular in cerebrally strong Western environments, to lack clarity on the distinction between the gift of leadership and the gift of teaching and to therefore forfeit the blessings that come from thinking about these two gifts with greater distinction. Before arguing for distinction, let me talk about the way the two gifts overlap. When elders are teaching God's word, I think they are expressing spiritual leadership *indirectly* via their spiritual gift of teaching. Teaching is the main spiritual gift in play, but because leadership may broadly be defined as influence, and because their teaching is influencing people, then in that sense they are leading. But it is better to simply say they are teaching rather than leading, as that is the main thing they are doing and because it can obscure the *direct* spiritual gift of leadership.

Then, when an elder thinks up an imaginative and audacious plan to mobilize the congregation to a tangible initiative, and then not only persuades the elders and congregation of it but infuses them with faith, and successfully leads them in that project, that is an example of a leadership gift expressed in a *direct* way. Common sense tells us that something distinct from the gift of teaching is in play in that scenario, and we know from experience that good teachers are not necessarily good leaders, and vice versa. It is therefore no surprise that the Bible presents teaching and leadership as two distinct gifts:

- They are listed *separately* in Romans 12:6-8.

- "Teacher" is mentioned *separately* to the other leadership gifts in Ephesians 4:11-12.

- In 1 Timothy 5:17 Paul draws a distinction between leading ("ruling") and preaching and teaching.

By turning up the contrast between the two gifts the importance of both gifts come into sharper focus. Some churches with strong leaders seem to prioritize *leadership over teaching* in a way that neglects the word of God, and replaces theological truth with pragmatic programs and personality-based motivation-by-manipulation. To protest this tragedy, it is of course tempting to swing the pendulum too far and claim that *leading* is in fact synonymous with *teaching* God's word. Phrases are invented to support this narrative such as "Christ rules his Church through his word" and "Elders lead the church through the word of God." Whilst both statements are true, the way they are expressed lacks the nuance of recognizing the role of other God-given gifts that the Lord uses to guard, guide and govern his Church. If the local church was merely a flock in need of care, or a class in need of instruction, then conventional pastor-teacher activities would suffice. But if the local church is in fact God's army to push back darkness in neighborhoods and nations, then the catalytic spiritual gift of leadership is cardinal.

Of course, it is not possible to have too much of God's word in church leadership, but it is possible to have too little leadership in church leadership. Let me illustrate by considering four important aspects of church leadership:

Church strategy: Similar to the book of Acts (Acts 13:2-3; 16:6-12), elders periodically need to make major strategic decisions that are not spoken to directly by Scripture, such as launching a building fund, taking on a new member of staff, or planting another church. High levels of biblical knowledge do not necessarily help in making such extra-biblical decisions, and often teacher-types are not naturally decisive or courageous in these areas, or strong at casting vision and mobilizing people.

Winning the lost: Have you noticed how some of the "best taught" churches are ineffective in winning the lost, and some of the "worst taught" churches are highly effective in winning the lost? How can this be? It is to do with spiritual gifts. To be successful in evangelism, evangelistic and leadership gifts are needed. The teaching gift alone will not cut it. The congregation needs to be motivated towards evangelistic living, and clear leadership is required to organize a church around evangelistic goals. The *teacher-heavy-leader-light* eldership team bumbles along saying, "Even if we aren't growing from conversions, at least our people are well taught." Conversely, the *leader-heavy-teacher-light* eldership team bluster along saying, "Winning the lost is more important than molly-coddling the found."

Activating obedience: Jesus defined the goal of teaching as activating God's people to obedience (Matt. 28:20). The *teacher-heavy-leader-light* eldership team are usually better at explaining truth to their congregation than they are at activating them to obedience – biblical accuracy alone doesn't produce biblical action. Conversely, although the *leader-heavy-teacher-light* eldership team feeds their congregation less biblical truth, they manage to mobilize them to do a surprising amount with it!

Choosing what to preach on when: Imagine the local church mission had stalled, morale was low, and there was apathy and compromise in the congregation. The *teacher-heavy-leader-light* eldership team might say, "Well, let's just continue to faithfully stick to the three-year series we are doing in Romans, and if people leave or complain, it is proof we are faithfully preaching God's word." Conversely, the *leader-heavy-teacher-light* eldership team might respond, "Quick, let's do some pop-psychology series to bring in the crowds." However, a mature team of *teachers and leaders* would respond, "To jump-start life in our church again, we need *biblical nourishment and prophetic stimulation*. Therefore, let's take a break from Romans, and do a series in the book of Judges. Without compromising the integrity of the text, let's draw some poignant prophetic parallels from Israel in the time of the Judges to the current state of our church. And, let us enthuse our preaching in this series with faith, exhortation and application more than we have ever done before. We need our teaching and leadership gifts to flow together powerfully in this series."

Clearly, the gift of leadership in harness with the gift of teaching (and other spiritual gifts) enables an eldership team to bring both *stimulation and security* to their church. Quite often a lead elder will himself be a strong leader *and* teacher (maybe implied in 1 Timothy 5:17?), and his preaching and broader ministry will be a useful blend of the two gifts. However, I know of some lead elders who are stronger leaders than teachers, who wisely share the pulpit with a more gifted teacher(s), sometimes preaching less than some of the other elders. In situations where the lead elder is a strong teacher but weak leader, thought needs to be given to how to inject the gift of leadership into the life of the church. It might be best for him to become the teaching elder and allow someone with a broader leadership gift to take the helm.

AVOIDING LEADERSHIP EXTREMES

Leadership and followership become toxic when biblical exhortations about leading and following are either over-developed or under-developed. Keeping an eye out for the following imbalances should enable a healthy leadership culture in church:

Leaders are called to lead "with zeal" (Rom. 12:8)

- If this is *over-developed*, leaders become overly confident, unyielding, even heavy-handed. Mark 10:42-45 and 1 Peter 5:3 warn against leading in that manner.

- If this is *under-developed*, leaders become timid, even impotent, and under-lead their followers.

Followers should imitate their leaders (Phil. 3:17, 1 Pet. 5:3, 2 Thess. 3:7, Heb. 13:7)

- If this is *under-developed*, an important and healthy aspect of discipleship is missing, because we need to be taught both biblical truth *and* how to live it out.

- If this is *over-developed*, a copy-cat culture can develop around personality traits or specific life practices of leaders. This can foster a formulaic approach to Christianity. *In extremis*, a personality cult can develop.

Leaders are called to lead from amongst the people, and from within a plurality of leadership (Phil. 1:1)

- If this is *under-developed*, too big a gap can develop between the leader and followers, leaving the leader(s) vulnerable to pride, aloofness, and heavy-handedness, and leaving the followers vulnerable to passivity and abdication.

- If this is *over-developed*, a leadership gift can be stifled by the congregation or the leadership team.

Leaders and followers are called to relationships of genuine affection (1 Tim. 5:1-2, 2 Cor. 8:5, 1 Thess. 5:12, 1 Chr. 12:18, Heb. 13:17b)

- If this is *under-developed*, relationships between leaders and followers can become corporate and transactional.

- If this is *over-developed*, relationships between leaders and followers can become soulish and claustrophobic. Sentimentality around relationships can stunt evangelism and growth.

Followers should have confidence in (Heb. 13:17), respect and esteem (1 Thess. 5:12, 1 Tim. 5:17), and obey their leaders (Heb. 13:17)

- If this is *over-developed*, leaders can manipulate and disempower their followers. It can lead to pedestalization of leaders, blind trust and unnuanced submission.[56]

- If this is *under-developed*, followers can manipulate and disempower their leaders. It can lead to sabotage of healthy leaders, and healthy leadership endeavors.

REFLECTION

1. Have you ever experienced "the grotesque situation in which the church commissions and authorizes people to exercise a ministry for which they lack both the divine call and the divine equipment?" Briefly describe.

2. Have you ever experienced the trouble that can come from "gifting writing checks that character can't cash?" Briefly describe.

3. Do you feel you have the spiritual gift of leadership? What makes you feel that?

4. Are you more conscious or intuitive in your leadership? What about your lead elder? What are the pros and cons of that for the team?

5. In your own words, summarize the argument for the need for distinction between the gift of teaching and the gift of leadership.

6. Do you think your team is leader-heavy-teacher-light, or teacher-heavy-leader-light, or a good balance? If there is an imbalance, what steps would you recommend to remedy the situation?

7. How well do you think your eldership team, and your church as a whole, is doing at balancing the biblical exhortations concerning leading and following? Explain your perspective. If anything, what could be done to improve the balance?

Elders

PART 6

CHARACTER

Elders

OVERVIEW OF PART 6

I said in Chapter 1 that a deficit of character is probably the biggest reason for a scarcity of elders and for impotence amongst elders. I also said that I am delaying talking about character until near the end of the book in the hope the reader will have a graver understanding of the need for character in an elder. I do hope that is the case, as healthy relationships with each other, with the lead elder, and with various groups in the congregation are not possible without solid character, nor is effective shepherding, teaching, equipping and leading.

In these chapters, we will work our way through 1 Timothy 3:1-13, Titus 1:5-9, and 1 Peter 5:1-4. I encourage eldership teams to revisit these chapters together annually as a safeguard. I have bundled the plethora of character traits under the headings *leading yourself*, *leading your family*, and *leading your church*. Please note a few things:

- As Don Carson points out, the remarkable thing about these characteristics is how unremarkable they are. With the exception of "able to teach" they are characteristics that every Christian should aspire to. Elders are called to exemplify *basic* Christian character, and be examples not exceptions.

- The lists are not exhaustive. There are other characteristics in Scripture that obviously apply to elders.

- There is overlap between some characteristics, but where possible I have pressed for distinction.

- We are not told exactly how much of each characteristic is enough to be an elder, so we assume they refer to behavioral *trends*, and that being "above reproach" is a good measurement.

- I have included the characteristics of deacons from 1 Timothy 3. Surely elders should have these characteristics also, as is implied by the word "likewise" that bridges the sections on elders and deacons in 1 Timothy 3.

- These passages are about *defense* and *offense*. Defensively, they protect us from damaging ourselves and others. Offensively, they damage the kingdom of darkness. Basic Christian character, selfless living, and steady faithfulness in the same direction are Satan's kryptonite (Gal. 5:22-23, 6:9, Rev. 12:10-11).

1 Timothy 3:1-13

¹ The saying is trustworthy: If anyone aspires to the office of overseer, he desires a noble task. ² Therefore an overseer must be above reproach, the husband of one wife, sober-minded, self-controlled, respectable, hospitable, able to teach, ³ not a drunkard, not violent but gentle, not quarrelsome, not a lover of money. ⁴ He must manage his own household well, with all dignity keeping his children submissive, ⁵ for if someone does not know how to manage his own household, how will he care for God's church? ⁶ He must not be a recent convert, or he may become puffed up with conceit and fall into the condemnation of the devil. ⁷ Moreover, he must be well thought of by outsiders, so that he may not fall into disgrace, into a snare of the devil. ⁸ Deacons likewise must be dignified, not double-tongued, not addicted to much wine, not greedy for dishonest gain. ⁹ They must hold the mystery of the faith with a clear conscience. ¹⁰ And let them also be tested first; then let them serve as deacons if they prove themselves blameless. ¹¹ Their wives likewise must be dignified, not slanderers, but sober-minded, faithful in all things. ¹² Let deacons each be the husband of one wife, managing their children and their own households well. ¹³ For those who serve well as deacons gain a good standing for themselves and also great confidence in the faith that is in Christ Jesus.

Titus 1:5-9

⁵ This is why I left you in Crete, so that you might put what remained into order, and appoint elders in every town as I directed you— ⁶ if anyone is above reproach, the husband of one wife, and his children are believers and not open to the charge of debauchery or insubordination. ⁷ For an overseer, as God's steward, must be above reproach. He must not be arrogant or quick-tempered or

a drunkard or violent or greedy for gain, [8] but hospitable, a lover of good, self-controlled, upright, holy, and disciplined. [9] He must hold firm to the trustworthy word as taught, so that he may be able to give instruction in sound doctrine and also to rebuke those who contradict it.

1 Peter 5:1-4

[1] So I exhort the elders among you, as a fellow elder and a witness of the sufferings of Christ, as well as a partaker in the glory that is going to be revealed: [2] shepherd the flock of God that is among you, exercising oversight, not under compulsion, but willingly, as God would have you; not for shameful gain, but eagerly; [3] not domineering over those in your charge, but being examples to the flock. [4] And when the chief Shepherd appears, you will receive the unfading crown of glory.

CHAPTER 21

LEADING YOURSELF

He that would govern others, first should be the master of himself. – Philip Massinger

GENERAL CHARACTERISTICS

Self-controlled, upright, holy and disciplined (1 Tim. 3:2, Titus 1:8)

Harry Truman said, "In reading the lives of great men, I found that the first victory they won was over themselves ... self-discipline with all of them came first."[57] Self-discipline is a never ending endeavor, but before a man becomes an elder he needs a decent track record of self-control, or else he will be vulnerable to the inevitable increase in temptation that he will experience as an elder – "a man without self-control is like a city broken into and left without walls" (Prov. 25:28).

Self-control is at the heart of self-leadership, and self-leadership is a prerequisite to leading others. Jack Paar quipped that life was one long obstacle course, with oneself the chief obstacle. D.L. Moody admitted that he had more trouble with D. L. Moody than any other man alive. Paul exhorted the Ephesian elders, "pay careful attention to *yourselves* and to all the flock" (Acts 20:28), and charged Timothy, "Watch *your life* and doctrine closely" (1 Tim. 4:16 NIV).

How are we to grow in self-control? We can draw on two divine power sources. The first is the power of *the gospel*. When continuously believed, the truth of Christ crucified for us is a magnetic force drawing us to godliness (Titus 2:11-12). The second is the *Holy Spirit*. Walking in the fellowship of the Spirit douses the desires of the flesh (Gal. 5:18), and we even have access to a fruit of the Spirit called self-control (Gal. 5:23)!

Above reproach (1 Tim. 3:2, Titus 1:6)

Before honing in on some areas of life that could be open to blame, Paul throws down a general marker saying that an elder should be above reproach. I expect he mentions it first so it can act as a gauge for some of the following characteristics of which we may be unsure exactly how *much* is enough. If doing X opens me, my church or the gospel to legitimate reproach, then I should not do X. Paul is not calling for perfection, but he is setting the bar high.

Sober-minded/temperate (1 Tim. 3:2)

Sober-mindedness, or temperance in some translations, refers to being even-keeled, stable, not prone to extremes. It is unlikely to be a reference to alcohol because "not a drunkard" is mentioned in the next verse. Winston Churchill said of General Tudor who resisted the great German advance of 1918, "The impression I had of Tudor was of an iron peg hammered into the frozen ground, immovable."[58] This is what elders are to be: iron pegs in frozen ground, immovable. They should be temperate at all times, but especially in the storms of life. If those at the helm of the church are not in firm control of themselves they will make problems in the church worse rather than better. Temperate elders bring stability to the church, helping God's people fight the good fight of faith "one step at a time; one punch at a time; one round at a time."[59]

Not arrogant (Titus 1:7)

Arrogance is a formidable force of darkness, although it is illogical because in the cold light of day we have nothing to be proud about, yet as Spurgeon said, it is as pervasive as the "flies of Egypt!"[60] It is fertilizer for a host of poisonous weeds, including hypocrisy, judgmentalism, and foolishness. Arrogance distorts our sense of reality, and leaders living in unreality are dangerous. No wonder "God opposes the proud" (Jas. 4:6). In our quest for humility, we should look in the right places. We should start with the truth that we are created not creator, dust not divine. Then, we should remember that we are *simul justus et peccator* (simultaneously justified yet sinners). But may I offer a caution here, as I have noticed that the Enemy is skilled at hijacking this truth that should be a source of humility, and converting it into a source of pride. It is good to have moments of brokenness about your sin, but humility is not acquired by focusing on your sin as much as focusing on God's grace. Humility comes from "great is He" not "woe is me" because any self-focus will eventually result in pride. If you think that *the more you remember your sin the humbler you will become*, it is just a matter of time before you become proud about your humility, and you are back to square one! Humility comes from Christ-focus, from boasting in what He has done. Through Jesus *we are no longer sinners who sometimes act righteously, rather righteous ones who sometimes act sinfully*. Celebrating our new identity as righteous saints produces a *loathing of sin and a self-forgetfulness* that keeps us from turning in on ourselves in either despair or pride.

SPECIFIC CHARACTERISTICS

Not double-tongued (1 Tim. 3:8)

Double-tongued means being untruthful, duplicitous, or slanderous with words. This would include failing to do what you say you will do, exaggerating a situation, misrepresenting what a person said or how they said it or what they really meant, or leading a person to believe that you are happy with an outcome from a meeting but then leading someone else to believe that you are not. An eldership team is built on trust, and if an elder's yes doesn't mean yes, or no mean no, trust can be rapidly eroded (Matt. 5:37, Jas. 5:12).

Not quarrelsome (1 Tim. 3:3)

"The wisdom from above is first pure, then peaceable, open to reason, full of mercy and good fruits, impartial and sincere" (Jas. 3:17). Being quarrelsome means not being that! Quarrelsome means being unnecessarily argumentative, opinionated, or dogmatic. If you regularly assume the role of devil's advocate, or always need the last word, you might be drifting towards being quarrelsome. Robust debate is healthy, but that is different from interrogating an idea *ad nauseam*. Also, once a decision has been reached (even if contrary to your opinion), it is quarrelsome to continually remind everyone that you don't fully agree with that particular direction.

Some elders are light on social awareness when in heated debate, and may simply need coaching on how to phrase their position in less emotive ways. Or, they might dominate a discussion simply by talking too much, which makes them appear more quarrelsome than they actually are! Both of these behaviors can be easily corrected and are not the same as being quarrelsome. Similarly, some elders have a naturally inquisitive personality type, and might be trained in the workplace to be particularly critical in their thinking. Again, this is not necessarily being quarrelsome, but these brothers will need to be aware that they can sometimes appear quarrelsome without meaning to.

Not quick-tempered (Titus 1:7)

Quick-temperedness is often a result of idolatry of self, an idol that takes particular offense when things don't go the way it likes. Due to an elder's responsible position over others, the stakes involved in losing your temper are high. People can easily get hurt or disillusioned, and in their minds the hundred times you showed godly restraint may be eclipsed by the one time you didn't. Practically speaking, we can be more tempted to quick-temperedness if we are hungry, tired, sick or stressed, so self-awareness in those areas is important.

Not violent (Titus 1:7) but gentle (1 Tim. 3:3)

Violence, unless in a legitimate context of self-defense, defending the weak, or in the military, is inappropriate for a Christ follower and especially for a Christian leader. We should rather correct, restore and bear with one another in gentleness and love (Gal. 6:1, Eph. 4:2, 2 Tim. 2:25). In terms of discerning possible root causes behind violence, they are probably similar to those behind quick-temperedness, as violence is often a severe manifestation of quick-temperedness.

Not a lover of money (1 Tim. 3:3)

Later in the same letter Paul elaborates: "For the love of money is a root of all kinds of evils" (1 Tim. 6:10). The problem is not money *per se* but the *love* of money, which significantly stifles our progress as believers (Lk. 16:11). Tell-tale signs include worrying about personal finances instead of trusting God to provide (Heb. 13:5-6), trying to get rich quick (Prov. 20:21), and most obviously not giving consistently to the mission of God. Living free from the love of money doesn't mean you should be either poor or entrepreneurially unimaginative, but it means that money will serve you and not the other way round.

Money talks a big game to try and make us fall in love with it. It asserts God-like characteristics, claiming to be able to offer us prosperity, peace, joy and security. But don't be fooled, it is impotent to deliver. Actually, if you fall in love with it, it will give you quite the opposite – ruin and destruction (1 Tim. 6:9), piercings and pangs (1 Tim. 6:10), and uncertainty (1 Tim. 6:17). Peace and security are only to be found in Jesus, the Prince of Peace and the Rock of Ages. So, brothers, let us be content with what we have, for God will never leave us nor forsake us (Heb. 13:5-6).

Not greedy for dishonest gain (1 Tim. 3:8), not greedy for gain (Titus 1:7), not shepherding for shameful gain (1 Pet. 5:2)

It is interesting how both *greed* and *dishonesty* are mentioned in 1 Timothy 3:8. Both are wrong, and the second is usually produced by the first. Honest gain is not wrong, but *greed* for it is. It is appropriate that Christian leadership results in honest gain (1 Tim. 5:17-18), but not *shameful gain* acquired via greed or dishonesty, or through an unhealthy motivation for financial reward (2 Cor. 2:17, 1 Tim. 6:5, Titus 1:7). Elders are to be free from the love of money, content, trusting God, and a model of generosity. We are men who worship God not money (Lk. 16:13), and we prove it by consistently giving money away to God.

Not a drunkard (1 Tim. 3:3, Titus 1:7), not addicted to much wine (1 Tim. 3: 8)

John Stott believes that Paul is contending here for self-control not abstinence:

> [Paul] did not require them to be total abstainers, since Jesus himself turned water into wine and made wine the emblem of his blood. Yet there are strong social arguments for total abstinence, since much reckless, violent and immoral behaviour is due to excessive drinking. What Paul requires, however, is moderation, as an example of the self-mastery already mentioned, not least because pastors are invited to many social functions at which wine flows freely.[61]

I would add that moderation should not camouflage an unhealthy dependency – you may not be drinking too much, but you might be drinking too regularly. If you are not sure, go without a drink for a week or month just to check that you are in control, not the drink. Of course, elders who drink alcohol should not go near drunkenness, nor should they cause those of weaker self-control or weaker conscience in this area to stumble. They should remain above reproach in this regard, which may depend on local culture and context, as drinking wine for breakfast might be above reproach in France but not in Africa!

REFLECTION

You may answer these questions by yourself, or better still with one or more of your fellow elders. You might like to meet together as elders several times to work through them all, or just once to focus on a few of them. Don't rush. Be sure to encourage and commend one another for the characteristics they embody, and exhort one another gently in the areas that need particular attention or vigilance. Pray for each other. For each characteristic:

1. Read the comment and discuss.

2. Each share how you think you are doing with the characteristic, then encourage and coach one another as appropriate.

Elders

CHAPTER 22

LEADING YOUR FAMILY

If a preacher's household is not in order, he should travel at least five miles before he preaches, and when he gets there, he should say nothing. – C.H. Spurgeon

He must manage his own household well, with all dignity. … If someone does not know how to manage his own household, how will he care for God's church? (1 Tim. 3:4, 5)

Paul's logic is that those who lead in the "larger" house of the church should first succeed in leading in the "smaller" house of their home. Our family lives with us 24/7, so what better proof of our ability to lovingly lead and disciple than the state of our families? Interestingly, of all things that Paul could highlight, he mentions managing our households with *dignity*. Leading with dignity means leading in a poised, statesmanlike manner – not always easy to do with the multi-faceted stresses on modern households. But if a man can hold his poise and disciple his family unit through the strains of homework, holidays, hormones, and hospital trips, then he might well be suited to lead a local church as an elder.

In view of the references to an elder's wife and children, can unmarried men or married men without children be elders? I believe so for the following reasons:

- Although the Bible anticipates elders being married men with children, it doesn't forbid unmarried men or childless men from being elders.

- 1 Corinthians 7 makes a compelling case for the ministerial advantages that single people have over married people. It would be strange to deny an eldership team that benefit.

- It would be equally strange to say that Jesus and Paul could not be elders in view of their unmarried status. Indeed,

Paul seemed to be a functional elder in the local church in Antioch.

- Arguing from greater to lesser, it would be odd for it to be permissible for apostles (such as Paul) to be unmarried and childless, but not elders.

In my experience, unmarried elders greatly enrich the team and the church. Of course, if a single elder were to desire marriage in due course, he would need to approach marriage carefully. Assuming he wanted to continue as an elder, he would need to marry someone who fits the biblical characteristics of an elder's wife, and may need to be given a leave of absence from the eldership team for a season in order to enable him to build a firm foundation for his marriage.

The husband of one wife (1 Tim. 3:2, Titus 1:6)

This statement not only prohibits polygamy, but speaks to the importance of marital faithfulness. Marital unfaithfulness is seldom far behind marital unhappiness, so we may surmise this statement means an elder's marriage should be in a decent state, not perfect, but trending upward. It is important to proactively strengthen your marriage. Maybe do some kind of marriage booster once a year, such as a marriage course. Maybe build in a meal twice a year with an experienced married couple where the main agenda is to talk about your marriage. Critically, if you hit an issue get help before things escalate. And defend your marriage. Defend it from anything, even good things, that can gradually sap life from your marriage, such as career, ministry, children, hobbies, and so on. But don't get isolated. Healthy marriages need lots of connection with other people, and doing the right things in the right amounts will strengthen your marriage.

Their wives likewise must be dignified, not slanderers, but sober-minded, faithful in all things (1 Tim. 3:11)

It is important that elders' wives are women of character. We looked at these four characteristics in some detail in Chapter 16. By way of a brief reminder, elders' wives should be *dignified*, meaning worthy of respect. Not flawless, not idolized, but worthy of respect in the way they "do life." They should not *slander*, meaning they should speak in a truthful and measured way about people, even when they or their husbands are mistreated. They should be *sober-minded*, meaning their emotions and actions are regulated by Jesus more than people or circumstance. And they should be *faithful in all things*. Not perfect in all things, or better than the other women in the church at all things, but *faithful* in all things. This surely means being reliable as a wife and mother, as a church member, and in keeping confidences.

His children are believers and not open to the charge of debauchery or insubordination (Titus 1:6), keeping his children submissive (1 Tim. 3:4)

Paul charges elders to raise children who are *believers* in Jesus Christ. Although salvation is ultimately in the hands of the Lord not parents, the exhortation is clear: do all you can to help your children come to an authentic, personal, saving faith in Jesus. Moving from belief to behavior, Paul says our children should not be *debauched or insubordinate*. Debauchery refers broadly to immoral living, and insubordination to disobedience. Some churches *understate* the importance of these verses, content with elders setting a very low standard of parenting. Other churches *overstate* the importance of these verses, setting unreasonably high standards for elders and their children. I will speak briefly to each extreme:

Understating these verses: We can underplay the importance of parenting for several reasons. We might think that parenting is a mere add-on to our busy lives and ministries, rather than part of the essence. But Psalm 127:4 tells us that our children are arrows and parents are *warriors* not archery hobbyists – that doesn't sound like an add-on activity! Or, we might be tempted to think that the way we parent doesn't really qualify or disqualify us for eldership. It does. That is exactly what Paul is saying here. Or, we might simply lack discernment about what good parenting actually means. Our cultural trend of hyper-individualism seems to beguile otherwise quite discerning people into thinking that good parenting means giving your children virtually unlimited choice and virtually no firm direction. That will certainly lead to what Paul calls insubordination.

In terms of upskilling as parents, you could ask an experienced couple to coach you on parenting, maybe meeting up with them a couple of times a year. Also, try and do some kind of parenting booster once a year, such as attending a parenting course, or reading a parenting book together and actively implementing some ideas from it. You might like to read our three parenting books: *Raising Obedient Children*, *Raising Well-Mannered Children*, and *Raising Christian Children*.

Overstating these verses: At first glance, these provisos for eldership (raising believing and obedient children) can place undue pressure on the elder and his wife. In fact, some churches have taken this Scripture as an isolated imperative rather than interpreting it against other truths in the Bible, and as a result have become intense and judgmental about the parenting standards that those in eldership, or aspiring to eldership, need to attain. Here are several things to consider:

First, although Paul is rightly placing responsibility on the parents to raise believing children (see also Prov. 22:6), we also know from Scripture that ultimately we have no ability to convert anyone: the nature of salvation is that God alone draws people to salvation (Eph. 1:3-12, Jn. 15:16, Acts 16:4, 1 Cor. 12:3), and an individual needs to respond to God directly rather than via his parents. Therefore, we conclude that the issue must be more about the parents faithfully raising their children *in the way of the Lord* rather than actually about the children turning into adult believers.

Second, Paul's lesser-to-greater argument (1 Tim. 3:4-5) suggests that the issue is more the integrity of the parents than the response of the children, because even in the church good leadership can sometimes result in people not responding to God as they should.

Third, common sense and experience show us that "children will be children" and from time to time will throw tantrums, misbehave, and "backslide." Also, children are different and can respond differently to godly, consistent parenting. If an elder's children are struggling with either belief or behavior, our response should be, "Are you doing everything you can to wisely parent your children? How can we help you and stand with you?"

And fourth, the Bible does not specify the exact levels of belief and behavior that our children should have, nor does it give a cut-off age when children cease to be children, therefore we should be careful when appraising elders in this area of parenting. None of this is to suggest that Christian leaders and Christian parents should go unchallenged for unfaithful parenting, or that parents should not trust God and diligently labor in laying in godly habits and beliefs that will one day, we trust, be fully owned by them as individuals before God.

REFLECTION

You may answer these questions by yourself, or better still with one or more of your fellow elders. You might like to meet together as elders several times to work through them all, or just once to focus on a few of them. Don't rush. Be sure to encourage and commend one another for the characteristics they embody, and exhort one another gently in the areas that need particular attention or vigilance. Pray for each other. For each characteristic:

1. Read the comment and discuss.

2. Each share how you think you are doing with the characteristic, then encourage and coach one another as appropriate.

Elders

CHAPTER 23

LEADING YOUR CHURCH

Leadership is a potent combination of strategy and character. But if you must be without one, be without strategy. – General Herbert Norman Schwarzkopf, Jr

If anyone aspires to the office of overseer, he desires a noble task (1 Tim. 3:1)

This rich little sentence teaches us several things. We learn that elder is a recognized *office* in the church. Of course, elders should not be officious in spirit, but there is a definite office of elder. We learn that eldership is a *noble* task. The nobility of an elder's role is surely derived from the nobility of that which he leads – the church, the Bride of Christ, that Paul reminds the Ephesian elders was "obtained with his own blood" (Acts 20:28). And, we learn that it is good for a man to *aspire* to eldership. Some men come to aspire to eldership on their own. Others need someone to suggest the idea and then they rapidly develop the aspiration. Still others develop the aspiration gradually, usually whilst on an elder training track of some sort. I occasionally come across men who I am convinced are called and suited for eldership but who just can't seem to acquire any God-prompted sense of call to it. I respect that, because aspiring to eldership – being drawn in by the nobility of it – is a vital characteristic of an elder.

God's steward (Titus 1:7)

Everything we have, including life itself, is a gift from God, therefore we should regard our whole life as a stewardship from God. Then add to that the privilege of leading God's precious church, and we see why an elder must be fundamentally motivated as a steward. I once took a wedding where it was pouring with rain and muddy outside the church. I was moved watching how the bridesmaids selflessly got wet and muddy to ensure that the Bride didn't. They were clear in their minds that the day was about the Bride, not them. They were resolute in their endeavor to present a clean, dry beautiful Bride to the Groom, even if they got grubby in the process. About a week later I preached a message entitled "Elders are Bridesmaids." The Bride we serve belongs to Him. We are stewards of the Son of Man's wife. And, one day we will give an account to God for how we stewarded our responsibility as maids to his Bride (Heb. 13:7).

Not under compulsion, but willingly, as God would have you … eagerly (1 Pet. 5:2)

The motivation for eldership must be "I get to" not "I have to." If a potential elder is feeling coerced into eldership by anything other than a joyful desire to be obedient to God's call, then he should not become an elder. Elders ooze eagerness, and never give off the impression that they are doing the Lord or the Lord's people a favor. Being eager means always being ready to "step up to the plate." Being eager means having a really good reason to say no to a request to serve. Our God-fueled eagerness will see us through testing seasons and enable us to regard inconvenience as privilege. I love the example of the spiritual leaders in 1 Chronicles 9:22-34: "They would spend the night stationed around the house of God, because they had to guard it; and they had charge of the key for opening it each morning" (v. 27).

A partaker in the glory that is going to be revealed … you will receive the unfading crown of glory (1 Pet. 5:1)

Here is a mighty motivation to elder well: eternal rewards! God is so good that he gives us salvation as a free gift, and on top of that gives us the privilege and fulfillment of serving him, and on top of that gives us rewards for all eternity (Matt. 16:27, Mk. 10:21, 1 Cor. 3:11-15, Rev. 22:12). Fixing our eyes on eternal rewards helps us stay unattached to the temporary delights of this world and shapes the way we handle our money, time and energy. We can happily trade earthly loss for heavenly gain. Our unfading crown of glory motivates us to live and lead well on this fading earth. Let us think about eternity, talk about eternity, and elder on earth in anticipation of the unfading crown of glory in heaven.

Shepherd the flock of God that is among you (1 Pet. 5:2), [until] the chief Shepherd appears (1 Pet. 5:4)

Jesus is the Chief Shepherd and elders are his under-shepherds. This realization enables us to shepherd with peace, gentleness and confidence. Peace, because we can rest in the knowledge that the Great Shepherd is ultimately responsible for his flock. Gentleness, because one should always treat that which belongs to someone else with special care. And confidence, because we know that we have been commissioned by Christ himself to lead his flock.

Exercising oversight (1 Pet. 5:2)

Although the New Testament words for *elder, pastor, shepherd* and *overseer* all essentially describe the same thing, Peter's use of the word *oversight* highlights how elders oversee the church in all matters, both doctrinal and general. This means elders need to be "bigger picture" men who can effectively govern the whole, and avoid hobby-horsing on any one aspect of church life. It is fine for an elder to have some areas of specific interest and involvement so long as they do not compromise his oversight of the whole. For example, an elder especially strong in pastoral care should check this strength of his does not limit the expansionist endeavors of the church. Conversely, an elder with an expansionist leaning should make sure that he is not insensitive to the pastoral pressures that expansion can incur (Acts 6:1-7).

> **Able to teach (1 Tim 3:2), [holding] the mystery of the faith with a clear conscience (1 Tim. 3:9), [holding] firm to the trustworthy word as taught, so that he may be able to give instruction in sound doctrine and also to rebuke those who contradict it (Titus 1:9)**

Elders need to be *able to teach* people from the Bible and help them apply biblical truth to their lives. We need to know what we believe and why, what we don't believe and why, and then be able to transfer and apply truth to others, which sometimes involves contending for truth and rebuffing heresy (Titus 1:9). *Holding firmly* to the word means never tiring of the basic truths of the faith: "To write the same things to you is no trouble to me and is safe for you" (Phil. 3:1), and, "Therefore I intend always to remind you of these qualities, though you know them and are established in the truth that you have. I think it right, as long as I am in this body, to stir you up by way of reminder" (2 Pet. 1:12-13).

Being able to teach presupposes a decent level of doctrinal maturity and pastoral skill. 1 Timothy 5:17 implies that some elders will play a greater teaching role than other elders, but minimally, all elders should be able to teach in a small group and one-on-one setting.

Also note that Paul is concerned that we believe the deep truths of the faith *with a clear conscience*. Elders should believe what we believe because we really believe it for ourselves, not just "because that is the church's position." And once we believe them, we must "hold firm" to them.

Hospitable (1 Tim. 3:2, Titus 1:8)

There are two elements to hospitality. Firstly, hospitality is words, actions and attitudes of love and acceptance towards others, i.e. generally being warm and pro-active in friend-making, literally making people feel "at home" around you. And secondly, hospitality involves having people into your home. Tim Chester writes:

> If I pull down books on mission and church planting from my shelves, I can read about "evangelism journeys", "the full-matrix network", "missional matrices" and so on. I can look at diagrams that tell me how people can be converted

or discover programmes that tell me how churches can be planted. It all sounds very impressive; very cutting edge. But this is how Jesus describes his mission strategy. "The Son of Man came eating and drinking'" [Lk. 7:34].[62]

The call to hospitality is everywhere in Scripture (1 Pet. 4:8, 1 Tim. 5:9, Rom. 12:9-12, 16:23, Acts 16:14, Titus 1:6, Acts 2:43ff), particularly for elders. If the private homes of the elders are open and welcoming, then the public home of the church will be open and welcoming. If the elders are creating a family feel, then the church will feel like a family. Hospitality is a bulletproof way of keeping leaders down-to-earth and engaged with those that they lead, and, so long as it is deliberately inclusive of outsiders and newcomers, hospitality is a powerful evangelistic tool.

Not domineering over those in your charge (1 Pet. 5:3)

Domineering means being haughty, bossy, authoritarian, holier-than-thou, over-bearing, controlling or manipulative – the antithesis of being a father. Although elders are called and confident, they should not be these things. Regarding heavy-handed leadership Jesus simply said, "It shall not be so among you" (Matt. 20:25-26). We should let the word of God and the example we set "do the heavy lifting" and avoid bulldozing people with legalistic arguments or force of personality.

A witness of the sufferings of Christ (1 Pet. 5:1)

Although we are not personal witnesses of Christ's sufferings like Peter was, we too should be mindful of, and shaped by, Christ's sufferings. I believe this means cultivating a perpetual gratitude for the suffering of Jesus that facilitated the victory of the cross. This gratitude helps fuel a willingness to suffer on behalf of others. It helps empower us to servant-hearted, enduring, and empathetic leadership.

He must be well thought of by outsiders, so that he may not fall into disgrace, into a snare of the devil (1 Tim. 3:7), respectable … dignified (1 Tim. 3:2, 8)

In a similar vein to being *above reproach*, Paul says an elder should be respectable, dignified, and well thought of by outsiders, presumably referring to those outside the church. One might erroneously think that because elders lead the *church* then it is only the congregation's definition of *above reproach* that counts. Yet Paul, knowing that much of an elder's life and work should be lived evangelistically amongst unbelievers, stresses that an elder's evangelistic witness and reputation in the community matters. Paul then raises the stakes further by saying that the devil is actively working to snare elders into being disgraced. Although non-Christians may not agree with our beliefs, they should still think well of us. Before appointing someone to eldership, give his boss a call!

He must not be a recent convert, or he may become puffed up with conceit and fall into the condemnation of the devil (1 Tim. 3:6)

This is likely a contextual issue, as Paul sometimes seemed to appoint leaders quite quickly in a pioneering context (Acts 14:21-23). In a more mature context, leaders should be comparatively more mature. A recent convert may have bags of zeal, but not yet have bags of wisdom. It can take time to grow in wisdom, humility and theological conviction. I can clearly recall two separate instances where two incredibly impressive young converts burst through the ranks in our church. As tempting as it was to fast-track these men to eldership, we heeded this verse and didn't give them special treatment. Sadly, in both instances they both got proud and retreated from responsibility and into sin.

The Bible gives no minimum length that someone should be a Christian before becoming an elder, nor a minimum age. Things to consider include the maturity of the man, the cultural view of age and leadership, the average age of the people in the church, and the stage of the church; often a pioneering situation will better tolerate younger elders.

Being examples to the flock (1 Pet. 5:3)

Elders should be examples not exceptions. Being an example to the flock means modeling Christian maturity. Albert Schweitzer said that example is not the best way to influence others, it is the only way. Elders should act the same in public as they do in private, and be able to say, "Be imitators of us and of the Lord" (1 Thess. 1:6). To set an example, we need to live up-close-and-personal amongst our people (1 Thess. 2:8). Like Gideon, we need to be able to say to our troops: "Look at me, and do likewise" (Jud. 7:17).

And let them also be tested first (1 Tim. 3:10)

1 Timothy 5:22 says "Lay hands suddenly on no man" (KJV). Laying hands on is easy. Laying hands off is traumatic. Appointing elders and deacons should not be an exercise in guesswork. When the writer of Hebrews says that followers should "consider the outcome" of their leaders' way of life (Heb. 13:7), the outcome that he is referring to is a proven track record. How has his life turned out over a meaningful period of time? What is the fruit of his decisions? Jesus said in Luke 16:10-12 that if a man is faithful with little, then you can trust him with more, and that if he is faithful with another's things, then he can have his own, and that if he is faithful in things natural, then he can be entrusted with things spiritual. So don't rush a leadership appointment. Watch a little longer. Test a little more.

REFLECTION

You may answer these questions by yourself, or better still with one or more of your fellow elders. You might like to meet together as elders several times to work through them all, or just once to focus on a few of them. Don't rush. Be sure to encourage and commend one another for the characteristics they embody, and exhort one another gently in the areas that need particular attention or vigilance. Pray for each other. For each characteristic:

1. Read the comment and discuss.

2. Each share how you think you are doing with the characteristic, then encourage and coach one another as appropriate.

Elders

PART 7

REPRODUCTION

Elders

CHAPTER 24
APPRENTICESHIP

Then we did the math. We needed one batch of elders to maintain our church, another batch to enable future growth of our church, and a third batch to send out to plant or strengthen other churches. We needed triple the number of elders we thought we did. The world was our parish, and it needed more elders.

MOTIVATION

The first church I planted grew rapidly into the hundreds in just a few years. We only had three elders, but we managed okay. We knew the Great Commission was supposed to involve both our neighborhoods and the nations, but we had our hands full in our "Jerusalem" and therefore didn't give much thought to "Judea, Samaria, and the ends of the earth." I remember being quite proud about both our laser focus on our locale and our small eldership team. Yes, I was somehow proud about our small vision and small eldership team. At first, I didn't realize the two were connected.

Then, God spoke to us in a number of ways that resonated with John Wesley's sentiment about the world being our parish.[63] We felt convicted that we had allowed our passion for our "Jerusalem" to justify in our minds ignoring the other "three-quarters" of Jesus' commission in Acts. 1:8. We repented of our unbiblical small-mindedness. And then we did the math. If we were going to be responsible with our "Jerusalem" as well as reach out further afield, we needed one batch of elders to maintain our church, another batch to accommodate future growth within our church, and a third batch to send out to plant and strengthen churches. We needed *triple* the number of elders we thought we did. The world was our parish, and it needed more elders!

"Triple it" became our catch phrase. The general idea is to try to triple the size of every leadership unit in the church, from a single Small Group to the Eldership Team. Not one apprentice, but two. If an area of ministry in the church could be led by one person, we made sure it wasn't. We made sure it was led by a team of three: the leader, and two assistant leaders. Often the two new assistants looked nothing like leaders when we recruited them, but a year later they did. Our various leaders' gatherings tripled in size. The level of camaraderie and the spirit of "can do" rocketed. "Triple it" is by no means an exact science so things were messy, but we soon began to multiply. Twenty years on, I can confidently say that "triple it" has served us well, giving us capacity to grow and multiply ministry again and again in our local church, and through church planting and strengthening further afield. On average, I think we have planted nearly a church a year over these two decades, in the process sending out hundreds of leaders, and many of those churches have planted more churches.

METHOD

I suggest using some kind of elder training track (ETT). These can be done in a multitude of ways to best serve your context. They can be formal or informal, they can take a few months or a few years, and they can involve wives much or little. But however you do it, I have observed that fruitful ETT's involve three important things: *pre-selection, experiential training coupled with structured study*, and *clear expectations*. Let's look at each in turn.

Pre-selection

You can never guarantee that someone who starts the ETT will end up becoming an elder, but in view of the potential disappointment of not becoming an elder, try to only invite men onto the ETT who stand a decent chance of becoming elders. This means some "pre-selection" has to be done to discern whether a potential candidate has genuine eldership potential. Ideally, this is done without raising his suspicions or expectations. It can be as simple as observing him in ministry in the church and spending social time with him, or through a more structured approach such as inviting him to join your eldership meetings for your time of prayer for a few months, because prayer is a particularly helpful environment to get a sense of a man's heart and theology.

Once you feel reasonably confident that he is a suitable candidate, you could have a conversation with him to see if he aspires to eldership. If he does, you could either invite him straight onto your ETT, or you could invite him to take an intermediary step such as attending your elders' meetings for a few months. You might say to him something like, "We have been chatting as elders, and we are wondering if you have any aspirations towards eldership? If so, we would like to warmly invite you to join us at the next few elders' meetings to take a tentative look at the world of an elder. Would you be open to that? Even if eldership isn't for you, we would benefit from your perspective at our meetings, and hope that you would benefit too." If he is keen, then explain clearly that this period is *not* the start of the ETT, but simply a period of *exploration* for both parties. Explain that at the end of this period, he would only start the ETT if both he and the elders felt it was right. Clearly framing expectations at this point is very important.

Experiential training coupled with structured study

A strong combination for any training program is on-the-job training (experiential) and in-the-classroom training (theory). In terms of *on-the-job training*, I suggest inviting apprentices into the team rather than onto the team. Alan Frow explains:

> They get a look at how our team functions and the issues it generally deals with. They pray with us, observe us collaborating around pastoral, governmental and visionary matters, they are encouraged to listen and learn as well as give their perspectives ... we want to expose them to both the cost and community of eldership ... and all of this is done without any promise of becoming an elder.[64]

Having apprentices *in* your team is an efficient use of time and resources, because you are incorporating them into an *existing* rhythm of meetings, rather than adding a new one. You are exposing them to some of your strongest men in the church, which will no doubt be a hot-house environment and help these saplings put on a growth spurt. It is also stimulating for the elders, upgrading even the blandest of elders' meetings into an elder training event.

Opinions differ over *how much to involve* the apprentices in your eldership activities. Some teams only include them in certain aspects of team life. Others gradually increase their involvement over time. And still others include them in everything from the get-go. I generally favor the latter approach because I have noticed apprentices learn more about eldership in one "tricky" meeting than in many "normal" meetings. We want them at the meeting when I have blown it and need to apologize to the elders. We want them there when a non-staff elder confesses he watched porn on a recent business trip. We want them at the meeting where we decide to dump the agenda and worship and pray instead. We want them with us when we are at our wits' end, on our faces before God, and crying out for wisdom. We want them with us when we wrestle with team dynamics, and bring correction to each other. We want them in the discussions around sensitive pastoral issues whenever possible. But there is a *cost*. Some elders may feel like they are on show; others may miss the intimacy of the original group; and sometimes you have to go slower than you would like. As for me, I consider this a bargain price for the blessing of turning our eldership team, and our eldership meetings, into an elder-producing machine.

In terms of *structured study*, I recommend reading, writing, and discussion minimally around *theological* issues and *eldership* issues. There is an abundance of decent *theological* resources and courses available, and you can either register an apprentice elder on an existing theological course, or you can cobble together a selection of suitable theology books and develop your own theological training track for the apprentices. As much as there is an abundance of good theological material out there, there is a dearth of inspirational and practical eldership material, particularly that gets into the weeds on the various relational dynamics of eldership. I wrote this book to help remedy that, and have designed the book to help *potential elders* lay foundations and test their calling and *existing elders* strengthen their foundations and affirm their calling. I suggest apprentice elders read a chapter(s) and write answers for the questions in the reflection section at the end of each chapter. Then, they meet with an elder(s) to discuss their answers. Existing elders might like to do something similar themselves periodically as a refresher.

Clear expectations

It is also important to communicate clear expectations in the ETT phase. Two main things need to be said. First, that you expect *whole-hearted commitment* to all aspects of the ETT. It can be wise to build in an off-ramp after a couple of months in case it is not working for either party. Second, that you are making *no promises*. In view of the explicit warnings about first *testing* a man before making him an elder (1 Tim. 3:6, 10, 1 Tim. 5:22), he needs to be clear that you are not committing to ever making him an elder. And, if that is the case, he needs to graciously submit to that, and not hold a grudge. Explain the goal is to prepare him for whatever his calling is, whether eldership or not. Encourage him that even if he doesn't emerge as an elder, he will emerge a better man.

REFLECTION

1. Articulate your own motivation to see more elders reproduced.

2. Make a few observations about the challenges and benefits of pre-selection for an ETT.

3. Make a few observations about the challenges and benefits of experiential training to both the trainee and the eldership team.

4. What potential problems do you foresee if expectations are not clear throughout the training process? How do you think you would personally handle a scenario where at the end of the ETT the elders felt that you were not called to eldership?

Elders

CHAPTER 25

APPOINTMENT

We cannot make people into leaders. We cannot simply vote them into office. We can observe and note the grace of God on people. We can see the anointing and respect the gift of God. A church that honours God's gifts honours God, and experiences God's ongoing favour. – Terry Virgo

TERMINOLOGY

How should we describe the process and moment of a man becoming an elder? We could use the phrase "set apart" which was used for Barnabas and Saul in Acts 13:2, and by Paul in Rom. 1:1 and Gal. 1:15, although none of these were specifically about becoming an elder. However, depending on your context, "set apart" could be a slightly obscure phrase. We could use the term "ordination," because the King James Version of the Bible regularly translates the word *poieo* as "ordained" (e.g. Acts 14:23 and Titus 1:5), although in some contexts "ordained" implies endowment of special qualities, which can sound more superstitious than biblical. I prefer the term "appointment" as it is a commonly used Biblical term, and easily understood in most contexts. It is used about Jesus in Luke 2:34, Acts 3:20 and Acts 10:42; about the Twelve in Mark 3:14; about the seventy-two in Luke 10:1; about the seven in Acts 6:3; about Paul in 2 Timothy 1:11; and specifically about the appointment of elders in Acts 14:23 and Titus 1:5.

WHO SHOULD BE INVOLVED IN THE APPOINTMENT PROCESS?

Historically, church officers have been chosen either *hierarchically* or *congregationally*. The Roman Catholic Church and some Protestant denominations favor a *hierarchical model*, whereby the Pope (or equivalent) appoints the most senior tier of officers, who then appoint the next tier, and so on, and the congregation is not involved. Antithetically, in many Protestant denominations and churches the local congregation, or a representative group from the congregation, choose their leaders. A perfunctory glance at the New Testament seems to imply support for both models. Acts 14:23 tells us that Paul and Barnabas appointed elders in various churches, and Titus 1:5 records Paul instructing Titus to do the same in Crete. Neither account specifies that they involved the local congregations in the process, although neither says they didn't. Conversely, in Acts 6 we see the congregation participating in the process of leadership selection (v. 3 "pick out from among you"), and similarly in Acts 1:23 the wider group were involved in finding a replacement for Judas.

So, is the *hierarchical* or the *congregational* approach correct? Rather than argue one over the other, I prefer to approach the matter from a different angle. I think the Bible speaks of *five entities* who are ideally all involved in the appointment of a new elder: *God*, the *candidate*, the *elders*, the *congregation*, and *outside ministry*.

God

In Acts 20:28, Paul reminds the Ephesian elders that the *Holy Spirit* had made them overseers. This is significant. He could have mentioned any of the "human" groups, yet he underlined that *God* was the One who made them elders. This is consistent with broader Pauline theology about God being the giver of all spiritual gifts (1 Cor. 12:4-11, Eph. 4:11-12). This is an important starting point, as it means that the job of the other four groups is not to *choose and appoint* but *observe and affirm* who God has chosen and appointed. Terry Virgo explains:

> Throughout the Old Testament, God chose whom He would to lead His people. The same principle

applies in the New Testament church. Jesus, our ascended Christ, gave gifts. We cannot make people into leaders. We cannot simply vote them into office. We can observe and note the grace of God on people. We can see the anointing and respect the gift of God. A church that honours God's gifts honours God, and experiences God's ongoing favour.[65]

This affects the atmosphere around apprenticing and appointing elders. It means that, rather than vying for their own influence, the four human groups will greatly appreciate each other's perspective in trying to "observe and note" the grace of God on a man for eldership. Therefore, whatever the process is, and whoever is involved in coordinating the moment of appointment, the after-taste should be that *God has appointed* and *people have recognized* rather than the other way around.

The candidate

1 Timothy 3:1 says, "The saying is trustworthy: If anyone aspires to the office of overseer, he desires a noble task." Clearly, an essential step in the process is for the man himself to *aspire* and *desire* to be an elder. And, in view of the serious and absorbing nature of eldership, his wife should also be fully supportive.

The elders

There is no clear New Testament example of elders (plural) appointing an elder(s). The closest we get is 1 Timothy 4:14 and Titus 1:5. In 1 Timothy 4:14, Paul reminds Timothy of "when the council of elders laid their hands on you," although we are not clear whether this was appointing Timothy to eldership or to some other ministry. In terms of Titus appointing elders on Crete, although he was likely an elder in his local church, he seemed to be operating more as Paul's apostolic delegate in Crete. However, because elders govern the local church, they obviously need to be in full agreement about inviting others to join their governing team. And, who better to help discern whether a man is suited to eldership than existing elders?

The congregation

There is no clear New Testament example of the congregation appointing elders, either by themselves or in liaison with another group(s). As we have said, the closest we get is the *principle* of their involvement in leadership appointment in Acts 6:3 and Acts 1:23. Still, to my mind, several things dictate that the local congregation *has to be* involved:

- To impose leadership on a congregation without their consent is contrary to the familial nature of New Testament churches, and could feel over-bearing.

- Thinking of the characteristics of elders mentioned in 1 Timothy 3 and Titus 1, I can't imagine any group being better positioned to vouch for elder candidates than the local congregation who would have observed them up-close-and-personal over time.

- We have no reason to assume that the principle of congregational involvement in Acts 6 and Acts 1 is *not* one that carries over to eldership appointments in some way.

Outside ministry

In Acts 14:23, we read about Paul and Barnabas appointing elders in the churches that they had planted, and in Titus 1 about Titus appointing elders in Crete. Some read too much into these verses, claiming that only outside authorities may appoint local elders. Others read in too little, hastily dismissing the obvious role that extra-local ministry can play in helping appoint elders. In a church plant situation, the prospect of credible "outsiders" helping appoint the first batch of elders makes a lot of sense. Such "outsiders" are usually respected leaders from the church or movement that helped plant and nurture the new church, and can be invaluable in helping the fledgling congregation navigate such a novel process. But even in a church where there are already elders, outside perspective can only benefit the process. I have been involved in situations where a wise outside voice has given the local elders a vital perspective that either encouraged, delayed, or even halted the process. Sometimes the issue was the suitability of the man (or wife) in terms of biblical qualifications or general maturity, and sometimes it was more of a contextual query around his suitability in terms of the team or the church.

Where possible, it is best to involve trusted outsiders early on in the process, rather than the day before the actual appointment! Maybe he/they could be part of the ETT in some way, and get to know the elder candidates long before it is decision time. Some churches even collaborate around an ETT together, enjoying the benefits of cross-pollination and outside perspective, and facilitating a new generation of elders from different churches getting to know each other, and learning and growing together.

I don't think it matters much whether the elders, the congregation, or outside ministry initially propose a man for eldership, only that all three groups are meaningfully involved. That said, because the elders are the highest human authority in the church and therefore have the final say on who becomes an elder, it is usually best for the elders to propose a new elder (after an ETT or similar) and then for the congregation and outside ministry to affirm it. This reduces the likelihood of the awkward and potentially hurtful scenario of someone being proposed by one group then denied by another. Involving the congregation can be as simple as announcing that you are hoping to appoint so-and-so as an elder in a few weeks' time, and asking them to communicate endorsements to the elders in writing, and any concerns to the elders in person.

LAYING ON HANDS, AND PRAYER

When Jesus appointed the Twelve (Mark 3:14), and when Paul and Barnabas appointed elders (Acts 14:23), we are simply told that they were "appointed." That's it. Even other appointments, such as Barnabas and Saul being set apart for apostolic ministry are reported in an equally low-key manner (Acts 13:3). These minimalist, matter-of-fact descriptions of appointments leave us with latitude in how we choose to conduct the moment of appointment, but should make us wary of overly-elaborate ceremonies (although what is "elaborate" varies between cultures and contexts). We should also be wary of attributing too much significance to the actual *moment* of appointment. Remember, it is God who gifts and appoints and man who recognizes (1 Cor. 12:4-11, Eph. 4:11-12).

Having acknowledged the latitude we have in how we do the moment of appointment, for the following reasons I think Scripture does indicate that such appointments should involve *laying on hands*:

- The appointment of "the seven" in Acts 6, and the sending out of Barnabas and Saul in Acts 13, include laying on hands. Although neither of these were appointments to eldership, the Acts 6 appointment was for a serving role, in a sense "junior" to the role of elders, and, the Acts 13 appointment was for apostolic work, in a sense "senior" to the role of elders. Therefore, there is every reason to assume that laying on hands should be part of appointing elders.

- 1 Timothy 4:14 speaks about the council of elders laying their hands on Timothy. While we cannot be sure that this was his appointment to eldership, it does show elders setting a man apart for some form of leadership position with the laying on of hands. It would seem consistent then, for elders to lay hands on new elders.

- 1 Timothy 5:22 speaks of not laying on hands hastily. The preceding verses are about how charges should be brought against elders, so it is reasonable to conclude that appointment of elders involves laying on hands.

Some consider laying on hands nothing more than a visible act of commissioning and brotherly love. I think it is certainly no *less* than that, yet it is quite a lot more. In the New Testament, hands were laid on to impart blessing (Mk. 10:16), to heal (Lk. 4:40), to impart the Holy Spirit (Acts 8:17-19), to impart spiritual gifts (2 Tim. 1:6) and, as we have seen, to appoint men to leadership positions (Acts 6:6, Acts 13:3, 1 Tim. 4:14, 5:22). Therefore, I believe we should lay hands on new elders in faith, praying that God would *bless* them, give them more of his *Spirit*, and give them the *spiritual gifts* that they need to be an elder. Nevertheless, as Strauch stresses, "we are not investing them with priestly character or granting them exclusive ministerial rights to administer the sacraments and the Word."[66]

WHAT COULD THE MOMENT OF APPOINTMENT LOOK LIKE?

Summarizing what has already been said, appointments are best done in a *culturally appropriate manner*, in a way that leaves the *accent on God appointing* and man recognizing, and involves *laying on hands and prayer*. I would also encourage it to be done when most/all of the *church are present*, because it is a key moment in the life of not only the man but also the church. Beyond these principles, there is much flexibility. You can appoint one or more elders at a time. It can be done at a mid-week gathering or in a Sunday meeting. It can take ten minutes or an hour. You can have one person speaking, or many. In our context, we usually do elder appointments in a Sunday meeting, taking about 15 minutes to do it. It usually looks something like this:

> *Explain*: We briefly explain what we are doing along the lines of, "As you know, Henry has been prepared for eldership over the last year, and as elders we believe he would be a great addition to our team. A few weeks ago, we received overwhelming affirmation from you, our congregation, that the Lord is calling Henry to be an elder. Therefore, today, we will recognize what God is doing by

appointing Henry to eldership, and commissioning both Henry and Liz in their ministry partnership. Although we are not appointing Liz to eldership, their one flesh union makes her a vital part of Henry's calling to be an elder."

Affirm: We invite them to stand up front, and someone reads out some extracts from the feedback from the congregation, and then we have an elder commend and affirm Henry, and an elder's wife commend and affirm Liz.

Charge: We ask 2-3 people (maybe an elder(s), a congregant, and a respected outsider) to each "charge" Henry to various aspects of eldership.

Response/pledge: We invite Henry to take 1-2 minutes to respond. This is often a particularly moving moment as he expresses his gratitude to the Lord and his love for the people.

Laying on of hands, prayer and commissioning: We invite the elders and their wives, and any visiting elders from other churches, and any respected outsiders who have been helping with preparing and affirming Henry and Liz, and some representatives from the congregation (maybe their Small Group and close friends), to gather around and lay hands on the couple and pray for them.

CARING FOR THE CANDIDATE (AND HIS FAMILY) IN THE LEAD-UP TO THE APPOINTMENT

The period surrounding the congregational affirmation and the actual appointment is a key time for the candidate, and his wife if he is married. It can be an exciting and affirming time, or it can be a lonely and insecure period. It takes courage to want to become an elder, particularly when the congregation give their feedback to the elders on whether they think you are as called and capable as you think you are! To help support and prepare the candidate, his wife and any children, and also to prepare the church, you might consider doing some of the following things during this period:

- *If necessary, schedule contexts where members can get to know the person better.* This could range from interviewing him (and his family) in a Sunday meeting, to more intimate Q&A sessions.

- *Have some dedicated prayer for the candidate.* This could be a special prayer meeting, or you could ask your Small Groups to regularly pray for the candidate.

- *If the person has children, in an age appropriate way help them feel part of the process.*

- *As elders, stay close to them* and help them work through any last-minute doubts.

REFLECTION

1. Which phrase for "appointment" is most helpful in your context, and why?

2. Do you concur that involvement from all five "groups" is optimal? Elaborate.

3. What ingredients would you like to see in an elder appointment, and why?

4. Imagine that you are a congregant. Write out a one-minute charge to a new elder, urging him to lead you in a Christ-like manner.

5. Imagine that you are an existing elder. Write out a one-minute charge to a new elder, urging him to be a good elder.

6. Imagine that you are the new elder. Write out a one-minute response.

FORWARD!

Forward, I say men, Forward! – Derek Landman

My first eldership team consisted of myself, Scott Marques and Derek Landman. At the end of each elders' meeting, Derek would often put on a posh English accent and say, "Forward, I say men, forward!" and then walk out the door. At first it was a bit of joke. And then it became a bit of a ritual. Now it is legend. Twenty-five years on, I still say it in elders' meetings. Derek is still an elder in the same church and he still says it in elders' meetings. I think all eldership teams should regularly say it. Certainly, it is what I want to leave you with.

When I was visiting Australia, my father-in-law took me to hear former Australian cricket captain Kim Hughes giving a speech. After twenty minutes of amusing stories and anecdotes, he leaned into his lectern and bringing a note of gravity to the proceedings, reminded us of the two animals on the Australian cricket badge – the Emu and the Kangaroo. In his gravelly Aussie voice, he said,

> Few people realize that these are the only two animals in Australasia that cannot go backwards. They are physiologically incapable of going backwards. They were well-chosen. And I say to you tonight that it is un-Australian to go backwards!

For one very brief moment, I wished I was an Australian. Fortunately, the moment of insanity quickly passed (!) and yet the moment marked me. It is un-elder-like to go backwards. We strain forward to what lies ahead (Phil. 3:13). We press toward the goal of the upward call of God in Christ Jesus (Phil. 3:13-14). We lay aside every weight, and we run forward in the race (Heb. 12:1). We run to win (1 Cor. 9:24). We put our hand to the plow and we do not look back (Lk. 9:62). Like the four living creatures, we go straight forward, led by the Spirit, without turning (Ez. 1:12).

Brothers, the backward gravitational tug of discouragement and fear is immense. There is a satanic tractor beam trying to keep us from gospel advance. Recognize it and resist it.

Like Moses, we call God's people forward (Ex. 14:15). We know that the Lord is with us wherever we go, therefore we call God's people forward in strength and courage (Josh. 1:9).

"Be watchful, stand firm in the faith, act like men, be strong" (1 Cor. 16:13).

ENDNOTES

1. General Herbert Norman Schwarzkopf, Jr, quoted in James Charlton, *The Military Quotation Book* (St Martin's Press, 2002) p. 83.

2. E.H. Friedman, *A Failure of Nerve* (Seabury Books, 2007) Kindle Location 115.

3. James Stewart, *Heralds of God* (Regent College, 1946) p. 26.

4. Oswald J. Smith, *The Man God Uses*, (New York: The Christian Alliance Publishing Co., 1925) Kindle Loc 740-744, Kindle Edition 2013, Formatting by George Stahnke.

5. C.H. Spurgeon, Sermon: 'An All-important Question,' October 4, 1906, *Spurgeon's Sermons*, Volume 52:1906 (No. 3008). Available at: www.ccel.org/ccel/spurgeon/sermons52.xli.html

6. R.K. Hughes, *Colossians and Philemon: The Supremacy of Christ* (Crossway Books, 1989) p. 45.

7. Ann Voskamp, *One Thousand Gifts* (Zondervan, 2010) p. 154-155.

8. Amy Carmichael, 'Hast Thou No Scar?' in Amy Carmichael, *Gold Cord: The Story of a Fellowship* (SPCK, 1952) p. 64.

9. Alexander Strauch, *Biblical Eldership* (Lewis and Roth Publishers, 1986) p. 154.

10. "Leaders" are mentioned three times in Hebrews 13. Those mentioned in v. 7 are possibly in prison (note the reference to those in prison in v. 3), but the leaders mentioned in v. 17 and v. 24 appear to be very much in circulation. Although these leaders are not referred to as elders, "perhaps they were leaders in the wider city church … at any rate, the leaders carried a weighty responsibility; they were accountable for the spiritual well-being of those

269

placed in their care" (F.F. Bruce, *The Epistle to the Hebrews* (Rev. ed.) (Wm. B. Eerdmans Publishing Co., 1990) p. 385. Their ministry of the word and watching over souls certainly sounds like the work of elders. If it walks like a dog, and barks like a dog…

11. Technically, it's the word most often used to translate "*presbuteros*," which is the word most often used to describe those who carry this role.

12. Timothy played the role of apostolic delegate in other churches before arriving in Ephesus, which would be consistent with him playing that role in Ephesus. And, at the end of 2 Timothy Paul says, "come to me," implying Timothy was not based at Ephesus permanently.

13. Strauch, *Biblical Eldership*, p. 33.

14. Bruce Stabbert, *The Team Concept* (Hegg Bros., 1982) p. 25-26, quoted in Strauch, *Biblical Eldership* p. 36.

15. Jeramie Rinne, *Church Elders* (Crossway, 2014) p. 86-90.

16. *Ibid*. p. 93.

17. Andrew Wilson, 'Is Eldership Gender-Neutral?', Think Theology blog, July 27, 2018. https://thinktheology.co.uk/blog/article/is_eldership_gender_neutral_a_response_to_katia_adams

18. Kathy Keller, *Jesus, Justice and Gender Roles* (Zondervan, 2012) Kindle Location 366.

19. I am referring to one to three leaders/elders of other churches who are known and trusted by the elders, maybe from within the association the church is part of. There might also be some key leaders within the local congregation, maybe senior deacons, who also provide meaningful counsel to the elders.

20. Group think is a psychological phenomenon where a group tries to reach a consensus without sufficient evaluation of alternative viewpoints, usually by isolating themselves from outside influences.

21. When the tallest "poppies" are recurrently pruned to the average opinion of the team and mediocrity becomes the new normal.

22. Rinne, *Church Elders*, p. 92.

23. Credit to Ger Jones (Vintage Church, LA) and Alan Frow (Southlands Church, CA) for this grid.

24. See Wikipedia www.en.wikipedia.org/wiki/Primus_inter_pares

25. Colin Baron, *Newfrontiers Magazine*, 2003.

26. Strauch, *Biblical Eldership*, p. 364.

27. *Ibid*, p. 362.

28. *Ibid*, p. 355.

29. A phrase from the Church at Brook Hills, Birmingham, Alabama. www.brookhills.org

30. For example, (1) John Stott, *The message of Romans: God's good news for the world*, (InterVarsity Press, 2001) p. 393; (2) Douglas Moo, *The Epistle to the Romans* (Wm. B. Eerdmans Publishing Co., 1996) p. 914; (3) Leon Morris, *The Epistle to the Romans* (Inter-Varsity Press, 1988) p. 528–529.

31. For example, see (1) Craig S. Keener, *The IVP Bible background commentary: New Testament*, (InterVarsity Press, 1993) 1 Tim. 3:11; (2) Philip H. Towner, *The Letters to Timothy and Titus* (Wm. B. Eerdmans Publishing Co., 2006) p. 265–266; (3) John Stott, *Guard the truth: the message of 1 Timothy & Titus* (InterVarsity Press, 1996) p. 101.

32. John R.W. Stott, *Guard the Truth: The Message of 1 Timothy & Titus* (InterVarsity Press, 1996) p. 101.

33. Craig Roberts, '10 Things I've Learned From Lambs', Modernfarmer.com; December 3, 2013. https://modernfarmer.com/2013/12/10-things-learned-lambs

34. *Ibid*.

35.   For example, if a congregant thought I was heavy-handed and unapproachable, then it would be uncharitable of me to expect the person to approach me about it. Although it might be biblically accurate (Matt. 18) to insist they do, the biblical atmosphere is one where the stronger do all they can to bear with the weaker.

36.   Juvenal, from his *Satires* (Satire VI, lines 347–348).

37.   Andrew Murray, *Teach Me To Pray* (Bethany House, 2002) p.103.

38.   See Roberts, '10 Things I've Learned From Lambs', *op. cit.*

39.   'Philosophy and Practice of Pastoral Ministry,' February 2014, Covenant Life Church, Maryland, Internal Paper, by DeVries, Maresco, Rogers and Wikner.

40.   Phil Newton, *Elders in Congregational Life: Rediscovering the Biblical Model for Church Leadership* (Kregal: Grand Rapids, 2005) p. 42.

41.   Handley Carr Glyn Moule, *Charles Simeon* (Methuen & Co., 1892) p. 87, quoted in David R. Helm, *Expositional Preaching* (Crossway, 2014) p. 12.

42.   Donald Coggan, *Stewards of Grace* (Hodder & Stoughton, 1958) p. 46.

43.   Tim Keller, *Center Church* (Zondervan, 2012) p. 89.

44.   The meta-narrative of the Bible is the good news (gospel) that through Christ's life, death and resurrection, God is graciously renewing all things, starting with those who believe in Jesus Christ.

45.   Martyn Lloyd-Jones, quoted by R.T. Kendall in Greg Haslam (ed.), *Preach the Word!* (Sovereign Word, 2006) p. 17.

46.   Greg Haslam, in Haslam (ed.), *Preach the Word!* p. 31.

47.   C.H. Spurgeon, quoted in Ray Comfort, *Spurgeon Gold* (Bridge-Logos, 2005) p. 104.

48. John Piper, Sermon: 'Alone in a Big Church,' September 20, 1981. Available at www.desiringgod.org/messages/alone-in-a-big-church

49. John MacArthur, Jr., Sermon: 'Characteristics of a True Church, Part 4', May 26, 2013. Available at www.gty.org/library/sermons-library/90-459/characteristics-of-a-true-church-part-4

50. John Calvin, *Commentaries*, Hebrews 10:24.

51. Timothy George, 'The Priesthood of All Believers,' First Things blog, October 31, 2016. www.firstthings.com/web-exclusives/2016/10/the-priesthood-of-all-believers

52. Carlyle Marney, *Priests to Each Other* (Judson Press, 1974) quoted by Timothy George in 'The Priesthood of All Believers', First Things blog, October 31, 2016. www.firstthings.com/web-exclusives/2016/10/the-priesthood-of-all-believers

53. *Ibid.*

54. John R.W. Stott, *God's New Society: The Message of Ephesians* (IVP, 1979) p. 165.

55. There are pros and cons to intuitive and conscious leadership styles. When it comes to decision-making, the "sixth sense" of intuitive leaders often enables them to make good decisions quicker than conscious leaders, yet they are often weaker than conscious leaders at *building sustainably* on those decisions. When it comes to *reproducing leadership*, intuitive leaders can be weaker than conscious leaders because they are harder to imitate, although they tend to *attract more high capacity followers* due to their greater flair. Following intuitive leaders can be an *exciting yet exhausting* ride, whilst following conscious leaders can sometimes not be exciting enough, but at least there's no danger of motion sickness.

56. The word of God must remain a higher authority than leaders. If your conscience is seared by your leaders, either resolve the matter or be free to move on without fear of vilification.

57. Harry Truman, Truman University Website, Truman Quotes page. www.truman.edu/about/history/our-namesake/truman-quotes

58. Quoted in Normal Vincent Peale, *The Power of Positive Thinking* (OM Books International, 2016) p. 157.

59. Rocky Balboa, in the movie *Creed* (Metro-Goldwyn-Mayer Pictures, 2015).

60. C.H. Spurgeon, Sermon: 'Pride and Humility', August 17, 1856, quoted in *The Complete Works of C.H. Spurgeon*, Volume 2: Sermons 54-106, Sermon 97.

61. John R.W. Stott, *Guard the truth: the message of 1 Timothy & Titus* (Downers Grove, IL: InterVarsity Press) p. 96.

62. Tim Chester, 'Eating together as enacted grace #1', 6 November 2007. Available at: https://timchester.wordpress.com/2007/11/06/eating-together-as-enacted-grace-1/

63. John Wesley, *Journal*, June 11, 1739.

64. Alan Frow, Southlands Church internal *E+ Expectations* Document.

65. Newfrontiers Magazine, Volume 2, Issue 04, Sept-Nov 2003, p. 7.

66. Strauch, *Biblical Eldership op. cit.*, p. 324.

CPSIA information can be obtained
at www.ICGtesting.com
Printed in the USA
LVHW081539090621
689799LV00017B/1034

9 781916 369160